THE FORMATION

OF SOULS

THE FORMATION
OF SOULS

Imagery of the Republic in Brazil

José Murilo de Carvalho

Translated by Clifford E. Landers
Foreword by Maria Alice Rezende de Carvalho

UNIVERSITY OF NOTRE DAME PRESS
NOTRE DAME, INDIANA

Published by the University of Notre Dame Press
Notre Dame, Indiana 46556
www.undpress.nd.edu
All Rights Reserved

Manufactured in the United States of America

First published in Brazil as *A formação das almas* by Companhia das Letras,
1990. Copyright © 1990 by José Murilo de Carvalho.

Library of Congress Cataloging-in-Publication Data

Carvalho, José Murilo de.
[Formaçao das almas. English]
The formation of souls : imagery of the Republic in Brazil /
José Murilo de Carvalho ; translated by Clifford E. Landers ;
foreword by Maria Alice Rezende de Carvalho
p. cm.
"First published in Brazil as A formaçao das almas,
by Companhia das Letras, 1990"—T.p. verso.
Includes bibliographical references and index.
ISBN-13: 978-0-268-03526-6 (paper : alk. paper)
ISBN-10: 0-268-03526-1 (paper : alk. paper)
1. Brazil—Politics and government—1889–1930.
2. Republicanism—Brazil—History. 3. Politicians—Brazil—
Attitudes—History. 4. Emblems, National—Brazil—History.
5. Brazil—Civilization—French influences.   I. Title.
F2537.C3613 2012
981'.05—dc23
2012023060

*The Brazilian Ministry of Culture provided support
for the translation and publication of this volume.
We are grateful to Francisco Weffort for his support
while he was Minister of Culture.*

*Daniel E. Colón, Julia Sendor,
Scott Mainwaring, Esther Terry, and Rebecca DeBoer
helped edit the translation and prepare the manuscript
for publication, and Stephen Little helped bring it
to fruition.*

CONTENTS

FOREWORD

The book that is now arriving in the hands of English-language readers was first published in 1990 and in the following year received the Jabuti Prize, the most prestigious literary award in Brazil. Since then, it has become indispensable to an understanding of Brazil. *The Formation of Souls* owes its success not only to the originality of its research and its analytic consistency but also to its place within the larger body of work of José Murilo de Carvalho, an author with one of the most consistent and celebrated research agendas in Brazil.

The first fruits of that agenda date back to the early 1980s, when Brazil underwent a slow political liberalization after twenty-one years of military dictatorship. In that context, reflection on the history and nature of the country changed course, although it still focused on questions formulated back in the 1960s. The prevailing debate targeted the local vicissitudes of capitalism and the key institutions in the social and historical formation of Brazil, namely, the large landowners (*latifúndio*) and slavery. It granted little protagonism to politics or politicians. The publication of *A construção da ordem: A elite política imperial* (The Construction of Order: The Imperial Political Elite) by José Murilo de Carvalho contributed a different perspective to the debate.

Originally part of Carvalho's doctoral thesis in political science at Stanford University, *A construção da ordem* was hailed by specialists for its important and innovative analytical approach to the Brazilian empire. With the publication nearly ten years later of the second part of his dissertation, entitled *Teatro de sombras: A política imperial* (Theater of Shadows: Imperial Politics), it was clear to an audience much wider than the narrow circle of specialists that José Murilo de Carvalho had produced a new interpretation of the foundations of modern Brazil. In this second book, economic factors were taken into account; however, they were no longer treated as determining the form of organization of power or the political decisions of the imperial elites. Instead, the author analyzed the political experience of the empire through the actions of its elites and not through an inevitable evolution of its structures. This book was translated into French and published by Maison des Sciences de l'Homme, Paris, in 1990.

With earlier editions sold out, and given the overwhelming demand for these two books from the university public and other readers interested in the political and historical trajectory of Brazil, they were at last published together in 1996. Perhaps one of the secrets behind the immediate enthusiasm of the general public for this combined volume was the fact that, with Brazil engaged in building a democracy in the 1980s and 1990s, José Murilo de Carvalho proposed a reflection on the quality of the Brazilian decision-making elites. He availed himself, nevertheless, of historical reasoning, that is, of a language that presented in a penetrating and nonjudgmental way the challenges put before us as Brazilian citizens.

The work of José Murilo de Carvalho on the Brazilian empire brought him immense popularity, both within the university system and beyond it. I once witnessed a scene uncommon among academics: in a small restaurant where professors and graduate students gathered in the Botafogo neighborhood of Rio de Janeiro, a regular customer approached the table where José Murilo was seated and respectfully asked him for his autograph on a paper napkin, emphasizing his admiration for the author and the pleasure that he derived from reading Carvalho's work. It was an educational experience for those of us who were there and knew how to interpret that gesture.

Carvalho's relationship with the general public had already been tested earlier, in 1987, with the publication of *Os bestializados: O Rio de Janeiro e a República que não foi* (The Bestialized: Rio de Janeiro and the Republic That Never Was). That book explored another universe of inquiries, opening a new page in his research agenda. The subject tackled this time was the Republic of Brazil in its inaugural hour. Carvalho analyzed the republic from its margins, that is, from the perspective of the men and women, free and poor, who in practice were not included in the new institutional game. He studied the city of Rio de Janeiro in its various dimensions: as the federal capital and therefore the stage for official policies and political practices, not always legal; as a space for the cultural affirmation and political exclusion of the common people; and as an environment in which the new economic elites began to experiment with the modern rules of sociability ushered in with the *belle époque*.

When *Os bestializados* was launched, conditions in Rio de Janeiro were foreboding. The city was in the midst of a large mobilization for urban and social reform. The indices of violence in the city were alarming, and the forces that were supposed to break the cycle of violence were incapable of stopping it, whether due to lack of preparation, omission, or corruption. The dramatic nature of the problem uncovered an image of Rio de Janeiro that its inhabitants did not want to face: at the close of the twentieth century, immense areas of the city were untouched by the rule of law. The population living in these areas were subject to violence and to the decisions of local bosses. It was as if the scenes presented by José Murilo de Carvalho in his most recent book had become visible to all citizens. In that context, *Os bestializados* assumed a different and unexpected dimension. By shedding light on certain aspects of the sociopolitical evolution of the city, ones that could still be detected and deplored a century later, the book helped fan the flames of ongoing debates over urban politics and planning and contributed to a developing social awareness.

By the time *A formação das almas* (*The Formation of Souls*) was published, José Murilo de Carvalho had already firmly established his research agenda in the minds of Brazilians. He was widely acclaimed as a leading scholar who easily explained the results of his work and who moved with equal dexterity in the academic world and in countless forums on issues of public interest. The launch of *A for-mação das almas,* therefore, was surrounded by the kind of expecta-tions that frequently accompany the presentation of new items in a beloved series, and it fully lived up to the enthusiasm of its readers.

This book, published in 1990, was conceived during the bicen-tennial commemoration of the French Revolution and the centen-nial of the Republic of Brazil, both of which took place in 1989. For that reason, it discreetly holds a double attraction, which helped to heighten interest in the book. It is a substantively Brazilian book, one characterized by native themes and characters, albeit one that may also be described as French, that is to say, in line with an ap-proach embraced by the best strain of historiography practiced in that country. On the one hand, the questions addressed in *The For-mation of Souls* continue and delve even deeper into the themes laid out in Carvalho's earlier works, principally in *Os bestializados.* On the other hand, the selection of the documentary corpus and the treat-ment were highly innovative in the Brazilian university environment. Nothing of the kind had ever been done before in Brazil.

The Formation of Souls is one of José Murilo de Carvalho's great-est books. Its author is a mature writer who comfortably navigates the academic environs and public debate in Brazil and is therefore capable of experimenting, of practicing what someone has called the "hermeneutics of forms," backed up by extensive republican iconog-raphy. Furthermore, this work established an esteemed political sci-entist as equally a historian—an uncommon occurrence, given the disciplinary boundaries that divide Brazilian universities. Because of its quality and impact, the book was also translated into Spanish and published by Universidad Nacional de Quilmes, Buenos Aires, in 1997.

This sophisticated work is predicated on one simple question: If the population of Brazil participated so little in the proclamation of the republic, what allowed the new government to consolidate itself? To answer that question, the author, in another pioneering exercise of Brazilian historiography, gathers together and rigorously analyzes a collection of the symbols, images, and allegories that populated turn-of-the-century Brazil. According to Carvalho, the political elites in Brazil realized that in order to *form souls,* it was necessary to put into action much more than good but erudite political doctrines. The distance that separated popular experience from the concept of a republic, whether that concept was formulated by liberals, positivists, or Jacobins, was vast. It was difficult to avoid simply giving in to the inability to establish communication between the two worlds. But if ordinary citizens were not to be formed by these doctrines, what would form them? Carvalho's response is that the early republicans tried to present their ideas in ways that were neither conceptual nor doctrinaire, by applying them in political cartoons, pamphlets, and monuments, and also in procedures and institutions. These republicans produced, or tried to produce, a pedagogy not derived from books but rather attuned to emotion. Nevertheless, the republicans did not achieve their objectives. As the author puts it, republican symbolism, with no roots in the collective experience, fell flat. For Carvalho, this is our contemporary challenge: the political, theoretical, moral, and even historiographical challenge of a social affirmation of the republic.

Carvalho's research agenda has remained consistent with that diagnosis. His 2001 book *Cidadania no Brazil: O longo caminho,* for which he received the Casa de las Américas prize, which included a Spanish translation—one of the most distinguished awards in Latin American culture—is essential reading on citizenship in Brazil. In addition to his numerous books, his body of work also includes countless articles and essays, which continue to give accurate and accessible meaning to political notions that, like the concept of a republic, may not be part of the daily vocabulary of the ordinary person.

A member of both the Brazilian Academy of Letters and the Academy of Sciences, José Murilo de Carvalho is one of Brazil's greatest intellectuals. A wider public deserves to see for itself.

Maria Alice Rezende de Carvalho,
Professor of Sociology, Catholic University of Rio de Janeiro,
and former president of the National Association of Research
and Graduate Study in Social Sciences, Brazil

Translated by Matthew J. Treme

ILLUSTRATIONS

For figures 1 to 37, see the indicated pages.

ACKNOWLEDGMENTS

I would like to thank the Research Institute of Rio de Janeiro (IUPERJ) in the Cândido Mendes University and the Rui Barbosa Foundation for their ongoing support. The IUPERJ receives substantial support from the Society for Financing Research Projects (FINEP), as well as from the Ford Foundation.

From an intellectual standpoint, first and foremost that I am indebted to Eduardo Silva, from the History Program of the Rui Barbosa Foundation. Several ideas presented in this book, especially those developed in the second chapter, resulted from our extensive conversations. The original project was intended to be coauthored; however, that was not possible because Eduardo traveled to England for his doctoral studies. I hope that he does not feel overly betrayed by the final product.

Some of the chapters were presented at conferences in Brazil, France, and the United States, and were shaped by the comments of colleagues whose names I could not keep track of—I gratefully thank you.

In the Rui Barbosa Foundation, my colleagues in the History Program discussed the initial project, and their suggestions have been incorporated. In particular, I would like to thank the interns Sueli Alves Henderson and Luciana Pazito Alves. They searched tirelessly through libraries and archives for obscure pieces of information and also offered valuable ideas and suggestions. Marson Jorge V. Alves helped complete the archival research.

The iconographic portion of the book was a collective effort by various people and institutions. I mention their names, apologizing ahead of time in case I accidentally omit any. To identify and reproduce paintings, photographs, political cartoons, and other objects, I had the invaluable assistance of Ângela Pôrto from the Rui Barbosa Foundation, and Cristina Barbosa, with whom I discovered the archives of the Positivist Church of Brazil. The magazines *Veja,* by way of Mário Sérgio Conti, and *Ciência Hoje* were generous in granting copyright permission. The following institutions, thanks to their directors and staff, made possible the task of identifying and reproducing material from their archives: the Positivist Church of Brazil, the National Museum of Fine Arts, the National Museum of the Republic, the National Historical Museum, and the Historical Museum of the City of Rio de Janeiro.

Chapters 4, 5, and part of 6 were written while I was a visiting professor in the History Department at the University of California, Irvine. I would like to thank Professor Steven Topik for his invitation and generous hospitality during my stay.

INTRODUCTION

My earlier study of the founding of the Republic of Brazil in 1889 demonstrated the absence of popular participation in its proclamation and the defeat of efforts seeking this participation in subsequent years.[1] Yet certain questions remained unanswered. Could the new regime have consolidated itself solely on the force of the oligarchic order? Could it not have undertaken, as almost all regimes do, attempts at legitimization to justify itself at least to the politically mobilized sectors, if not to the entire population? If so, what were those efforts, what means did they utilize, and what were the results?

The classic instrument of legitimization for political regimes in the modern world is ideology and its rational justifications of the organization of power. In Brazil, at least three ideologies competed to define the nature of the new regime: American-style liberalism, French-style Jacobinism, and positivism. These three fought each other intensely in the republic's nascent years, until liberalism claimed the victory around the turn of the century.

The ideological justifications, although fundamentally discursive in nature, also possessed elements that went beyond the merely discursive or the scientifically demonstrable. They posited models for the republic and models for the organization of society in which utopian and visionary aspects were embedded. Jacobinism, for example, idealized classical democracy. Direct democracy, or government by means of the direct participation of every citizen, was its ultimate goal. For liberalism, the utopian ideal was a society where the invisible hand of the market harmonized the interests of autonomous individuals. In this vision of society, the government should interfere as little as possible in citizens' lives. Positivism possessed even more obvious utopian elements. It viewed the republic in a broader perspective that postulated a future golden age, in which human beings would achieve their goals in the bosom of a mythic humanity.

As discourse, republican ideologies remained cloistered within circles of the educated elite. But, whether because of the content of the discourse itself or the utopian elements, these ideologies ended up going beyond the restricted world of the elites, and they came to defend, each in its own way, popular involvement in political life. This was clearly the case of the Jacobins, whose direct inspiration was the French Revolution. At the time of the proclamation of the Republic of Brazil, the French Revolution was the most powerful example of the explosion of the common people. In some respects, this was also true for the orthodox positivists. Although they theoretically opposed revolutionary movements, they held the Revolution of 1798 to be a watershed in the history of humanity, and they had a communitarian and inclusionary vision of the ideal society. On a lesser scale, the liberal model could also include demands for broader popular participation. Because these ideologies permitted or even demanded an expansion of popular participation, I discuss them in chapter 1.

I am directly concerned with the expansion of imagery of the republic to the world beyond the elite, or with attempts at such an expansion. This expansion was nearly impossible through a discourse that was unintelligible to a public with a low level of formal education, so it would have to be achieved by more universal, more accessible means, such as images, allegories, symbols, and myths. A preliminary examination of the actions of Jacobins and positivists in fact had already revealed to me the use of such means, often under French influence. Descriptions of the period bear reference to Brazilian republicans' custom of singing the *Marseillaise* and of representing the republic as wearing a cap of liberty; they also relate the positivists' struggle over the new flag and the dispute centered around defining the civic pantheon of the new regime.

After further research, I verified that there was also among us Brazilians a battle of symbols and allegories, albeit on a lesser scale than in the French case, which nevertheless became an integral part of the nation's ideological and political battles. This battle revolved around the images of the new regime, and it sought to reach the popular imagination in order to re-create it within the framework of republican values. The battles for the popular republican imagination will be the central theme of this book. The elaboration of a collective imagination is an integral part of the legitimization of any political regime, for through this collective imagination one reaches not only the head but especially the heart, or the aspirations, fears, and hopes of a people. Through this collective imagination, societies define their identities and objectives and their enemies, and they organize their past, present, and future.[2] The social imagination is constituted and expresses itself undoubtedly through ideologies and utopias, but also—and this is what interests me—through symbols, allegories, rituals, and myths. Because of their diffuse character and their relatively uncodified reading, symbols and myths can become powerful elements for projecting interests, aspirations, and collective fears. To the degree that they are successful in reaching the imagination, they can also shape worldviews and serve as models of conduct.[3]

Manipulation of the social imagination is especially important at moments of social and political change, which can redefine collective identities. The French Revolution, throughout its several phases, is a classic example of the attempt to manipulate collective sentiment in order to create a new political system, a new society, and a new human being. Mirabeau said it succinctly: It is not enough to show the truth, it is necessary to make people love it, it is necessary to take control of the imagination of the people.[4] For the French revolutionaries, public education aimed, above all, to shape souls. In 1792 the propaganda section of the French Ministry of the Interior was appropriately named the Bureau de l'Esprit.

The work of Jacques-Louis David (1748–1825) as painter, revolutionary, and art theorist is the best example of the effort at civic education through the use of symbols and rituals. Mainly due to his painting *The Oath of the Horatii* (1784), he was one of the principal representatives of classicism during the French Revolution. For David, however, classicism was not merely a style or an artistic language. It was a vision of the world as a set of social and political values based on the simplicity, nobility, and civic spirit of the old republics, encompassing the Spartan austerity and the sacrificial dedication of Roman heroes. According to this vision, the artist uses his art to spread these values.[5]

By 1792 the painter had been elected a member of the French National Convention and participated in the Committee for Public Education and Fine Arts. He was deeply involved in redefining cultural policy, reforming art salons, and producing symbols for the new regime. Most important, he designed the tricolor flag and organized the great ritual of the Festival of the Supreme Being in 1794. He presided over the committee chosen by the National Convention to select the jury that served in the 1792 exhibition. In this capacity, David presented to the Convention a report (if not written, then certainly influenced by him) that established new directives for artists and new ideas on the nature and role of art. According to this report, "The arts are an imitation of nature in its most beautiful and perfect aspects; a natural feeling in man attracts him to the same objective." Further, the arts should inspire grand and useful ideas. Art should not only enchant the eyes but, above all, strongly contribute to public education by penetrating into souls, for "the characteristics of heroism, of civic virtues, offered to the eyes of the people electrify their souls and bring forth the passions of glory and of devotion to the happiness of their country."[6] David was perhaps the first to perceive the importance of using symbols in constructing a new set of social and political values.

The French Revolution is notorious for its production of symbols, which were indeed varied and extensive: from the tricolor, the emotionally charged *Marseillaise,* and the cap symbolizing liberty to the feminine image, the tree of liberty, and the egalitarian greeting "citizen." They included the 1792 revolutionary calendar, created to mark the advent of a new era, and the great civic festivals such as those of the Federation in 1790 and the Supreme Being in 1794. Various minor symbols and allegorical images, such as the scale, the level, the rudder, the spear, the Gallic rooster, the lion, and so forth, also contributed to the era's extensive utilization of symbols. Despite varying degrees of acceptance and a hostile reception by enemies of the French Revolution, the revolutionaries employed these symbols exhaustively. A true battle of symbols, resulting from the revolutionary waves between 1789 and 1871 and at the whim of monarchical and conservative reactions, was waged in the attempt to conquer the social imagination throughout a century of French history.

The Brazilian republicans, turning to France for inspiration, found a plethora of materials at their disposal. The Brazilian liberals could not garner the same symbolic wealth from their model, the United States. This lack of competition facilitated the republicans' success with revolutionary symbolism. For reasons beyond the scope of the discussion here, the American Revolution was much less prolific than the French in producing revolutionary symbols, perhaps because of a lesser need to win the hearts and minds of a population already converted to new values. The "American" liberal movement in Brazil also showed little interest in promoting a popular republic or expanding political participation beyond the necessary minimum. It limited itself to an ideological battle, insisting on its version of the myth of origin of the new regime and its represented figures: the founding fathers. As such, the battleground remained almost unobstructed for the actions of the "French" republicans.

Among the propagandists in Brazil, enthusiasm for France was undeniable. The fact that 1889 was the centennial of the 1789 French Revolution served only to increase it. Silva Jardim openly preached the overthrow of the *ancien régime* in Brazil, to coincide with the centennial. He outright referred to shooting Count d'Eu, a Frenchman who had landed the role of the hapless Louis XVI in a tropical replay of the drama of 1792. The enthusiasm was best expressed in the words of a naval officer, who in 1912 recalled the times of propaganda: "All our aspirations, all the concerns of the propaganda republicans were actually copied from French traditions. We spoke of beloved France; of the influence of French culture; in the smallest aspects of our political struggle we recalled France. The *Marseillaise* was our battle hymn, and we knew the events of the great revolution by heart. Our cry 'Long live the Republic!' was almost always followed by 'Long live France!' . . . France was our guide; we spoke of her always and under any pretext."[7]

More than the *Marseillaise* was borrowed from France. Even before the proclamation of the new government, the allegorical representation of the republic as a woman was already widely accepted; the cap of liberty invariably appeared, covering the female figure's head or held in her hand. "Citizen" became a title—citizen president, citizen minister, citizen general; it replaced the solemn, imperial, Catholic "May God protect your Excellency" in official correspondence. "Health and Brotherhood" became part of discourse.[8] Jacobins and positivists were prominent in this effort, with the latter group's characteristic specificity related to the historical, philosophical, and religious views of Auguste Comte, and with their own conception of the political strategy to promote social transformation in Brazil. Both groups proved their awareness of the importance of using symbols and myths in the battle for the triumph of their version of the republic.

In this book, I discuss in depth the content of some of the principal symbols used by Brazilian republicans and evaluate their acceptance or rejection by the public, that is, their efficacy in promoting the legitimization of the new regime. This discussion of symbols and their content may provide valuable elements for understanding the proposed visions of the republic and of society, history, and human beings themselves. It can help reveal the divergences and conflicts among the different concepts of the republic at the time. The acceptance or rejection of the proposed symbols may reveal the preexisting republican roots in the popular consciousness and the capacity of the manipulators of symbols for remaking that consciousness in accordance with new values. A symbol establishes a meaningful relationship between two objects, or two ideas, or between objects and ideas, or even between two images. Although the establishment of that relationship may begin with an act of will, its acceptance and its political efficacy depend on the existence of what Bronislaw Baczko has called a community of imagination or a community of meaning.[9] If this common terrain does not exist, whether in the roots of the pre-existing imagination or in collective aspirations in search of a new imagination, the relationship of meaning is not established and the symbol becomes empty, if not a laughingstock.

Among the various symbols, allegories, and myths that were utilized, some seem more obvious and more capable of casting light on the phenomenon of the Brazilian republic and its founding. Each of these will be the subject of a separate chapter. Chapter 2 discusses the myth of origin of the republic. The creation of an origin myth is a universal phenomenon found not only in political regimes but also in nations, peoples, tribes, and cities. Often disguised as historiography, or perhaps inextricably intertwined with it, the origin myth seeks to establish a version of the facts—real or imagined—that makes sense of and gives legitimacy to the winning side. In the case of the creation of new regimes, the myth establishes the truth of the winning side against the forces of the past or of the opposition. If not openly distorted, the facts behind the mythicized version of a truth acquire dimensions that successfully convey the desirability and superiority of that version. Individuals involved undergo the same distortion.

Chapter 3 deals with the myth of the hero, also of long-standing history. Every political regime seeks to create its civic pantheon and emphasizes figures that serve as images and models for members of the community. Although heroes can be completely mythological figures, in modern times they can be real people. However, the process of creating heroes necessarily includes the transmogrification of a real figure in order to turn him into an archetype of collective values or aspirations. Some attempts at constructing heroes fail because of the real figure's inability to lend himself or herself to such a transformation. In some situations, the same figure can present different hero-images to different sectors of the population, as in the case of Abraham Lincoln. To the black population of the United States and to the East Coast in general, Lincoln was the hero-savior of the people, a martyr. To the Midwest and West, he was the hero-conqueror, the pioneer, and the frontiersman.[10] Because he is in part real, in part constructed, and the result of a process of collective elaboration, the hero conveys less about himself and more about the society that produces him.

One of the most popular allegories of the republic in France was the figure of the female. The inspiration was found in Greek and Roman antiquity, in which female divinities represented ideas, values, and feelings. Pallas Athena was the goddess of wisdom in war or peace, and could also appear as the goddess of victory; Aphrodite was the goddess of love, fertility, and beauty; Ceres, the goddess of the harvest and abundance.[11] The Brazilian republicans tried to employ the same symbolism. The acceptance of the feminine symbol in France and its rejection in Brazil allows, through comparison and contrast, for the clarification of different aspects of the two societies and the two republics. This will be the theme of chapter 4.

In modern times, certain national symbols, such as the flag and the anthem, are virtually obligatory. They have become official identifications of nations. All of these symbols possess a history, although not always a peaceful one, that is nearly always linked either to the birth of the nation or to the establishment of a political regime. Embodied with strong symbolic power, some flags and anthems have traversed national borders. In the year of the proclamation of the Brazilian republic, such was the case for the *Marseillaise,* a symbol not only of the Revolution of 1789 but of every revolution and liberation movement in the West. The history of anthems and flags thus constitutes another analytical instrument for exploring the value, the content, and even the ideological content of political regimes, if not of entire societies. Chapter 5 discusses the flag and the anthem.

Finally, a separate chapter is devoted to the orthodox positivists, who were the most articulate symbol manipulators of the new regime, surpassing the Jacobins in organization and perseverance. Bearers of an integrated worldview, including an operational code and well-defined political tactics, the orthodox positivists best understood the importance of symbolic manipulation in the reconstruction of the social imagination. Their inspiration in a philosophy that was somewhat alien to Brazilian culture, yet balanced by an emphasis on the value of tradition, contributed to a mixture of successful and failed outcomes. Here, too, the limitations of voluntarism in the manipulation of the collective imagination and the importance of the community of meaning are clear.

chapter one

REPUBLICAN UTOPIAS

Benjamin Constant's lecture in 1819 at the Athénée Royal in Paris, entitled "On the Liberty of the Ancients Compared to That of the Moderns," serves as a point of departure for discussing republican models at the end of the nineteenth century. In this lecture, the thermidorian Constant, an enemy of both the Jacobins and Napoleon, attributed the evils of the Revolution of 1789 to the influence of philosophers such as the Abbé de Mably and Jean-Jacques Rousseau, who defended a type of freedom no longer adaptable to modern times.[1] This freedom, also adopted by the Jacobins, characterized the ancient republics of Athens, Rome, and especially Sparta. It was the freedom to participate collectively in government and sovereignty; it was the freedom of the public man. In contrast, the freedom of the moderns, which suited the new times, was the freedom of the private man: the freedom of the right to come and go; the freedom of property, of opinion, and of religion. Modern freedom includes the right of political participation, now executed by representation rather than by direct citizen involvement. The development of commerce and industry, Constant argued, would no longer allow people the time to deliberate in the public square, nor were they interested in doing so. Today, people seek personal happiness and individual interests. Political freedom serves to guarantee civil freedom.

This opposition between two types of freedom and two ways of conceiving the political organization of a society was also present during the American Revolution of 1776, where revolutionaries clearly opted for the modern freedom. The Brazilian republicans, who at the end of the nineteenth century struggled to justify the new regime, could not escape such a debate. Embodied in the idea of a republic, themes regarding the interest of the group, the individual, the nation, and citizenship were central concerns of the builders of the Brazilian republic. As a country that exported raw materials and imported ideas and institutions, the existing models of a republic from Europe and America, especially the United States and France, served as Brazil's constant points of reference. This chapter discusses how these models were interpreted and adapted to local circumstances by the republican political elite.

The Two Freedoms

The founding fathers of the first great modern republic, the United States of America, considered the concept of the republic ambiguous. Alexander Hamilton observed that, until then, the concept was applied to very different forms of government. It was applied to Sparta, where senators were in office for the duration of their lives; to Rome, even under the kings; to the Netherlands, which had a hereditary nobility; and to Poland, which had both an aristocracy and a monarchy.[2] "Republic" could mean free government, as well as government by law and popular government. However, the founders, or the great majority of them, were certain of one thing, namely, the philosophical basis of their undertaking, or the basis of the new political pact under which individual interest and the quest for personal happiness predominated. Hume's utilitarianism was the source of common inspiration for all. To Hume, all men were knaves and could be motivated only by an appeal to their personal interests. It was, therefore, a matter of a concept of freedom that was perfectly adapted to the moderns' notion of freedom as described by Benjamin Constant. The utilitarian world is the world of passions, or at best, the world of reason at the service of passions; it is not the world of virtue in the old meaning of the word.

Utilitarianism, with its emphasis on individual interest, presented difficulties for the concept of the collective or the public. The most common solution was to simply define the public as the sum of individual interests, as in Mandeville's famous formulation: private vices, public virtue. In order to explain the undeniable fact that some people in certain circumstances were motivated by reasons other than simple material interest, Hamilton resorted to yet another passion: the love of fame and glory. Love could combine the promotion of private interest with the public interest. In any case, what appeared in *The Federalist,* as Gerald Stourzh has observed, is the vision of a nation without patriots and the vision of a collection of individuals in search of a political organization that would guarantee their interests. This vision does not include a collective identity, feeling of community, or feeling of country.

Setting aside the question of whether this view of a lack of collective identity among the inhabitants of the Thirteen Colonies was correct, the emphasis on the individual led the American founders to a particular concern for the organizational aspects of the new society. In the absence of affective ties of solidarity, it became more difficult to found the new political society solely on the calculus of interest. As Hannah Arendt observes in *On Revolution,* in America, a true revolution was already achieved before independence. The revolution was actually the new society planted in America. It was up to the founders to promote the *constitutio libertatis,* or the organization of freedom, more so than to make the declaration of freedom. Perhaps because of this, still according to Arendt, the American Revolution was the only one that did not devour its children and that succeeded in institutionalizing itself. The contrast with the French Revolution is telling: the declaration of freedom predominated, to the detriment of order. In the United States, Montesquieu was the most important author; in France, it was Rousseau. Institutional innovations, such as the separation of powers guaranteeing freedom, the bicameral legislature absorbing separatist forces, and the balancing power given to the Supreme Court, were largely responsible for the durability of the

American system. We will later observe how these innovations in political engineering appealed to Brazilian republicans.

The French provided another model for the republic. The republics of Spanish America were either considered derivatives of the American model or not classified as models at all because of their characteristically turbulent politics. To refer to "the French model" is incorrect, however, for there was more than one French model as a result of the vicissitudes suffered by that country's republic. The First and Third French Republics constituted points of reference for different publics.

The images of the First Republic became confused to some extent with those of the Revolution of 1789, or principally the Jacobin phase, in which the aspects of popular participation stood out. According to Benjamin Constant, this was the phase that most approximated the concept of freedom in the style of the ancients. It was the republic of the direct intervention by the people in government; the republic of popular clubs, great demonstrations, and the Committee of Public Safety. It was the republic of the great mobilizing ideas of collective enthusiasm, freedom, equality, and universal rights of the citizen.

The Third Republic, which demonstrated a reasonable capacity for survival, provided an alternative point of reference. Certain characteristics of the Third Republic pertained to the influence of the criticism by the liberal tradition of the Revolution of 1789 and of Benjamin Constant himself. Constant had already openly influenced the Brazilian imperial constitution in its adoption of the idea of a moderating power, which he called *pouvoir royal* or *pouvoir neutre*.[3] This was the idea of a power above the legislature and the executive that could serve as a judge of and a balance point for the constitutional system and that could be adapted by both constitutional monarchies and republics. Constant's concern was the governability of, and conciliation between, freedom and the exercise of power. According to him, this problem was not resolved in France by either the First Republic, which had too little government, or the subsequent empire, which had too little freedom. Making the republic governable was one of the principal worries of the leaders of the Third Republic. Constant, as someone too connected to the imperial tradition, could not serve as a source of inspiration for Brazilian republicans.

The model of the Third Republic, or rather a variant thereof, arrived in Brazil mainly through the mediation of both domestic and foreign positivists. The strong ties between French positivists and politicians of the Third Republic, some of whom were avowed positivists, such as Léon Gambetta and Jules Ferry of the so-called group of "opportunists," facilitated this transmission. The expression "opportunist" was coined by Émile Littré, the leader of the nonorthodox positivists. One of the central points of positivist political thinking, as expressed in the motto "Order and Progress" and supported by Benjamin Constant, was to make the republic a viable system of government. Or, in Jules Ferry's words: "The Republic must be a government."[4]

There were disagreements on how to make the Third Republic into a government. Positivism itself had multiple factions, such as the orthodox positivists of Pierre Laffitte's group, who did not accept the parliamentarianism adopted by the French constitution of 1875 and who were increasingly impatient with the delay in breaking off relations between church and state and with the timidity of educational policies. The orthodox faction still held on to the idea of republican dictatorship as developed by Comte. Littré himself was elected senator, and his group accepted parliamentarianism and admitted compromises on important questions such as church-state relations in the name of opportunism or, in positivist terms, in the name of the necessity to wait for a suitable sociological moment to intervene. In any case, both the orthodox and the heterodox factions found political inspiration in the *Appel aux conservateurs*, published by Comte in 1855. In this text, the concept of "conservative" came from Comte's particular view of the French Revolution, which sought to avoid the so-called metaphysical, Robespierrist/Rousseauist Jacobinism and also the clerical reaction favoring restoration. In Comte's view, a conservative was someone who succeeded in reconciling the progress brought by the French Revolution with the order necessary to hasten the transition to a normal society, or a positivist society based on his religion of humanity.

The major point on which orthodox positivism departed from the ideas of Benjamin Constant was its rejection of parliamentary government. This divergence was relevant for Brazilian republicans. Comte took his idea of republican dictatorship from Roman tradition and from the revolutionary experience of 1789, which were, incidentally, related. The expression "republican dictatorship" simultaneously implied the idea of a discretionary government of national salvation and the idea of representation and of legitimacy. It was not despotism. To Comte, Danton was a republican dictator and Robespierre a despot. But this idea remained ambiguous, to the extent that in the *Appel aux conservateurs,* Comte presented the legitimist Charles X as the best embodiment of the republican dictator.

Whatever the precise context of the expression, its consequences for the idea of representation and for the organization of republican policy were important. The idea of representation embedded in the figure of the dictator approaches symbolic representation or virtual representation. In these two concepts, the representative takes the place of the represented, in relation to which he possesses great independence.[5] The republican dictator, for example, would hold a lifetime office and could choose his successor. If he represents the masses in theory, he can distance himself from them in practice. In reality, the good Comtean dictator would be the one leading the masses. In the spirit of *Appel aux conservateurs,* the monocratic, republican, and conservative dictatorship has the clear sense of a government of order whose task is to bring about *d'en haut,* the transition to the positivist society. Republican dictatorship bears a similarity to the concept of conservative modernization espoused by Barrington Moore.[6]

Positivism, especially in Laffitte's version, possessed another characteristic that made it relevant to the discussion of Brazil's situation. We have mentioned the Hamiltonian ideal of a nation without patriots, to which was opposed the Rousseauist vision emphasizing the collective, the idea of civic virtue, and the public man. Comtean positivism introduced a variant of these two approaches. As is well known, Comte's work underwent a profound transformation after his meeting with Clotilde de Vaux in 1845. Religious elements came to dominate the scientific aspects; feeling was placed above reason and the community above the individual. According to his own account, Comte began to unite the social instinct of the Romans (civic virtue) with the affective culture of the Middle Ages, as expressed in the traditions of Catholicism. In this sense he departed completely from individualism, but he did not replace it with Rousseau's notion of the general will. To Comte, both individualism and the general will were metaphysical notions. Comteanism introduced forms of communitarian experience—the family, the fatherland, and, as the culmination of the evolutionary process, humanity (which Comte wrote with a capital *H*).

Comte's emphasis on the notion of the fatherland is especially important. The fatherland is the necessary mediation between family and humanity and the necessary mediation for development of the social instinct. To carry out this function, it must constitute a true community of shared life and therefore not possess an excessively large territory. The perfect fatherland should be characterized by the feminine traits of feeling and love. The good *patria* would be *matria*. Such a view, if incompatible with the idea of a nation without patriots, also parted ways with Rousseau's communitarian thought, which possessed contractual elements and therefore traces of individualism. The positivist citizen does not act in the public square, nor does he deliberate about public questions. He loses himself in the communitarian structures that absorb him completely.

Thus, at least three models of the republic were available to the Brazilian republicans. Although they started from totally distinct premises, two of these models, the American and the positivist, emphasized aspects of the organization of power. The third model posited popular intervention as the basis of the new regime, while disdaining the aspects of institutionalization. Although the idea of a republican dictatorship was used in French models, it remained vague in the Jacobin version, while the positivists specified in detail the role of dictator, of congress, electoral norms, and political education.

Politicians had already adapted American and European ideas and institutions during the period of the Brazilian empire. Even before the country's independence, colonial rebellions were inspired by the American or French Revolution. Importing models, or finding inspiration in external sources, was not exclusive to Brazilian republicans. The American founding fathers sought inspiration in ideas and institutions from antiquity, the Renaissance, and contemporaneous England and France. The French Revolution, in turn, had points of reference in the classical and in the American example. The phenomenon of looking for external models is universal. This does not mean, however, that it cannot be useful for understanding a particular society. Which ideas to adopt, how to adopt them, and which adaptations to make are concerns that may reveal the prevalent political forces and the values of the importing society.

The Imperial Legacy

The Brazilian empire achieved an ingenious combination of imported elements. Its political organization was inspired by English constitutionalism, via Benjamin Constant. For better or worse, the Brazilian monarchy experimented with a cabinet form of government and with national parties, elections, and a free press. Administratively, the inspiration came from Portugal and France, two countries most affiliated with the empire's centralizing policy. The statist bias of imperial politicians found French administrative law particularly attractive.[7] Finally, even certain Anglo-American formulas, such as the justice of the peace, juries, and limited provincial decentralization, served as references when the centralizing weight provoked strong reactions.

All of these imports served the central political concern, or the organization of the state in its political, administrative, and judicial aspects. Guaranteeing the survival of the country's political unity and organizing a government that could maintain the union of the provinces and the social order were the greatest priorities. Only toward the end of the Brazilian empire did questions and discussions arise regarding the formation of the nation and the redefinition of citizenship. One of the leading politicians at the beginning of independence, José Bonifácio, called attention to problems in forming the nation. He particularly mentioned the issues of slavery and racial diversity. But such issues remained secondary, for the most urgent task at hand was, purely and simply, the survival of the country.

After the consolidation of national unity in the mid-nineteenth century, the national theme was raised again, primarily in literature. *O Guarani,* a novel written by José de Alencar and published in 1857, sought to define a national identity through the symbolic linking of a young blonde Portuguese woman and a bronzed Indian chieftain. The union of the two races, in an exuberant tropical setting far away from any signs of European civilization, indicated a first attempt at sketching what would be the basis of a national community with its own identity. In the political sphere, the national theme was resumed only when the time came to face the problems of slavery and its correlate, foreign immigration. Affecting the various provinces in different ways, these problems reflected the problem of political centralization. The republicans had to confront these challenges. In fact, the option in favor of a republic and the model of the republic that was adopted reflected the desired solution to the problems of slavery and centralization.

Although the monarchy abolished slavery in 1888, its primary intention was to preserve public order, which was threatened by the mass flight of slaves and the economic demand for contract labor from coffee-growing regions. The social problem of slavery and the problem of incorporating former slaves into national life and into the very identity of the nation remained unresolved and were generally evaded.

The more lucid abolitionists and the reformist monarchists had proposed measures in this direction, such as agrarian reform and education for freedmen. But within the short space of the year between the abolition of slavery and the founding of the republic, nothing was done because the imperial government spent almost all its energy staving off attacks from former slaveowners, who were intolerant of abolition without compensation.

The Brazilian empire, on the other hand, had faced the problem of redefining citizenship in such a way as to impede the incorporation of the freed slaves. The electoral law of 1881, which introduced the single-round direct vote under the pretext of moralizing elections, drastically reduced electoral participation. The requirement that voters read and write reduced the electorate from ten percent to less than one percent of a population approaching fourteen million. Popular support for the imperial government, including that from the black population, was due more to the symbolism of the paternal figure of the king than to any actual electoral participation in the country's political scene.

The Republican Option

The republicans faced the task of replacing a government and building a nation. Each republican group, advocating varying solutions, faced the task differently. Schematically, three different positions can be distinguished.

The first position was that of rural landowners, especially that of the landowners in the state of São Paulo. Since 1873, the country's best organized republican party, which consisted mainly of landowners, was based in São Paulo. The province experienced a surge in coffee expansion, yet landowners felt smothered by monarchical centralization. For these landowners, the ideal republic was, without a doubt, that of the American model. The individualist definition of the social contract suited them. It avoided broad popular participation both in implementing and governing the Republic of Brazil. Furthermore, by defining the public as the sum of individual interests, it provided this group with a justification for defending their private interests. The *fin-de-siècle* version of the liberal posture was Social Darwinism, which was absorbed in Brazil through the intermediary of Herbert Spencer, who inspired Alberto Sales, the principal theorist of the republic from the state of São Paulo.

The American emphasis on the organization of power also suited São Paulo landowners not only because it was in the tradition of the country but especially because it was concerned with social and political order, and it was assumed to be a fitting cause for a class of former slaveholders. For the republicans of three major provinces

1. Alberto Sales,
ideologue of the liberal republic

of the empire—São Paulo, Minas Gerais, and Rio Grande do Sul—
federalism was perhaps the most important feature of the new regime; the American federalist solution especially suited them. Installation of a bicameral system was part of the federative solution to
console this group of landowners.

The American model, which was largely victorious in the 1891
Constitution, had a profoundly different sense from that which it
had in the United States, in spite of its appeal to the interests of the
rural landowners. As Arendt reminds us, the revolution in the United
States had already occurred through a new egalitarian society formed
by the colonists. The concern with organized power, as we have seen,
was more a consequence of the virtual absence of social hierarchies.
In Brazil, there was no prior revolution. Despite the abolition of slavery, society was characterized by deep inequalities and by the con-
centration of power. In these circumstances, liberalism took on the
character of embracing inequality and of sanctioning the law of the

strongest. Coupled with a presidential government, a republican Darwinism had at hand the ideological and political instruments to establish a profoundly authoritarian regime.

Certainly, this model did not meet the interests of those dissatisfied with the monarchy. For an urban sector made up of small property owners, liberal professionals, journalists, teachers, and students, the imperial regime seemed to limit employment opportunities. I say "seemed" because, although the imperial system was slow in promoting abolition, and its excessive centralization and the longevity of some segments of the political elite (lifetime senators, for example) were regarded as the causes of these malcontents' problems, the actual causes lay in other factors (such as slavery itself, which limited the labor market). As it happened, republican ideas conditioned the very evaluation of the monarchy. The Jacobins' evaluation, in particular, tended to project onto the Brazilian monarchy the same vices as those of the French *ancien régime,* however unjustified the comparison of the two realities. The Jacobins saw in the Brazilian monarchy, for example, backwardness, privilege, and corruption, which were surprising discoveries at a time when the emperor was one of the great promoters of the arts and science, when the nobility was merely titular and not hereditary, and when public morality was perhaps the highest in Brazil's history as an independent nation. But these accusations were probably made in good faith and were part of the republican belief system.

To the Jacobins, the orthodox liberal solution was unattractive, for under it, they lacked control of the economic and social resources that could afford them an advantage in a system of free competition. They were more attracted by abstract appeals for freedom, equality, and participation, although they were not always clear in what ways such appeals could be turned into reality. That very difficulty in visualizing how to realize them left them on the level of abstractions. The idea of "the people" was an abstract one. Many of their references were symbolic. The radicals spoke of revolution (they were eager for it to occur on the centennial of the great French Revolution of 1789) and of people in the streets. They called for the death of the prince-consort of the heir to the throne (who was a French noble!)

2. Silva Jardim,
advocate of the Jacobin republic.

and sang the *Marseillaise* in the streets. But had they attempted their
desired revolution, the people, who in Paris had taken to the streets
to storm the Bastille and sent kings to the guillotine, would not have
appeared. The sympathies of the dangerous classes in Rio de Janeiro
lay more with the monarchy than with the Jacobins. The Jacobin idea
of the equality of the citizen was adapted to the local hierarchies:
there was the citizen, the citizen-sir, and even the citizen-sir-general.

As such a solution was hardly plausible, the partisans of the old-
style freedom comprised a small, albeit aggressive, group. The majority of these malcontents perceived the difficulty, if not the impos-
sibility, of implementing the republic in the public square. They were
against the monarchical regime but not against the state, since it was
the most effective means of achieving their goals. Like the abolitionist Joaquim Nabuco, they understood that without the state, it would
be difficult to end slavery—the state's dark side. Disinterested in the

American solution and suspicious of the Jacobin one, this group sought another solution to the difficulty.

The positivist version of the republic, in its diverse variants, offered such a way out. The positivist theoretical arsenal was loaded with useful weapons, beginning with the condemnation of the monarchy in the name of progress. According to the positivist law of the three phases, the monarchy corresponded to the theological-military phase, which was to be replaced by the positivist phase, whose best embodiment was the republic. The separation of church and state was also an attractive feature for this group, particularly for teachers, students, and members of the military. By the same token, the idea of republican dictatorship and the appeal of a strong and interventionist executive served their interests well. Progress and dictatorship, progress through dictatorship, and progress by state action were ideals of enlightened despotism that had deep roots in the Luso-Brazilian tradition from the time of the Marquis of Pombal in the eighteenth century. And finally, the positivist proposals to incorporate the proletariat into modern society and to implement a social policy had greater credibility than an abstract appeal to the people, and they opened the way for the republican idea among the working class, especially state laborers.

A social group particularly attracted to that vision of society and republic was the military. The fact is extremely ironic, for according to positivist theses, a military government would be a social regression. Such surprises make the adaptation of ideas an interesting phenomenon. The military, unlike the civil elite with their literary background, had a technical background and consequently found the positivist emphasis on science and industrialization very attractive. Furthermore, because it was a part of the state, the military could not dispense with the state as an instrument of political action. The idea of republican dictatorship strongly appealed to members of the military, although in Spanish America it may have dangerously resembled a defense of the military caudillo; foreign observers, especially Europeans, saw it as such during the two military governments at the beginning of the Brazilian republic.

3. and 4. Miguel Lemos and Teixeira Mendes,
apostles of the sociocratic positivist republic,
Positivist Church of Brazil.

For specific historical reasons, the positivist model also seduced the republicans of Rio Grande do Sul. Perhaps the region's military tradition, the need of its republican minority for discipline and cohesion in order to impose themselves, and its less complex local society, compared to that of São Paulo or Rio de Janeiro, contributed to its more intense embrace of the political ideas of positivism. The state constitution of Rio Grande do Sul incorporated more positivist elements than any other state constitution, especially with respect to the dominance of the executive; the unicameral budgetary legislature; the lack of reference to God, who was replaced by the triad of family, fatherland, and humanity; and social and educational policy.[8]

Citizenship and Stateship

With the exception of the few radicals, the various groups that sought a way out for the monarchy through republican models, even those whose point of departure was based on liberal premises, ended up placing an emphasis on the state. This result was due, in part, to the country's long statist tradition, a mark of its Portuguese heritage reinforced by the imperial elite. In addition, the slavocratic society had few occupational niches, causing the jobless to turn to public employment or state intervention to provide career opportunities. Unemployed college graduates, military men dissatisfied with low pay and skimpy appropriations, state laborers in search of social legislation, and urban migrants in search of jobs—all looked to the state for their salvation. The entrance of all of these groups into politics came about more through the gateway of the state than through an affirmation of a right of citizenship. It was a means of entrance that may accurately be termed "stateship" rather than citizenship.

Although certain social obstacles to the Jacobin solution have already been mentioned, they merit expansion. The exercise of freedom by the ancients demanded republican virtue on the part of the citizenry, that is, a concern for the public good. Such a concern, however, is threatened whenever opportunities for enrichment increase, for then ambition emerges and social inequality develops. Republican virtue was a Spartan virtue. This theme, perceived earlier by Machiavelli, was reintroduced on the eve of the creation of the modern republics. In France, Montesquieu and especially Mably regarded a certain degree of social equality as a condition for civic virtue. Mably thought that only Switzerland met such a condition, since the United States was already corrupted by inequality. Jefferson, the most "ancient" of the founding fathers, also doubted the viability of civic virtue in the United States because of the growth of business and industry, both sources of corruption. On such a view, the patriot is virtually incompatible with the economic man; citizenship is incompatible with the economic culture.[9] That was in fact the position of Benjamin Constant, for whom the development of business and industry were the fundamental causes of the inadaptability of the old-style concept of freedom to the modern world.

Besides having emerged in a profoundly unequal and hierarchical society, the Brazilian republic was proclaimed at a time of intense financial speculation, caused by the government's issuing of money to meet the needs generated by the abolition of slavery. The resulting speculative fever especially affected the nation's capital city, the center of the events that led to the establishment of the republic. Instead of agitation by the Third Estate, the Brazilian republic was born in the midst of the agitation of speculators, agitation that the republic only increased by continuing the policy of printing money. The speculative spirit of personal enrichment at any cost was widely criticized in the press, from the pulpit, and in novels, and gave the new regime a stamp incompatible with republican virtue. In such circumstances, one could not speak of the utilitarian definition of the public interest as the sum of individual interests. There was simply no concern for the public. What prevailed was a predatory mentality, or the spirit of capitalism without the Protestant ethic.

The second military government, or the Brazilian republic's Jacobin phase, responded to the situation by attacking speculators and bankers and thus creating for itself a unique reputation. The most popular image of President Marshal Floriano Peixoto was as the guardian of the treasury—a pallid, tropical version of the Robespierre of the Committee of Public Safety, who had been known as the Incorruptible. But the response was short-lived. Corruption and shady dealing once again came to characterize the new regime, making its predecessor, an earlier target of corruption accusations, seem the picture of public austerity. Representations of the republic in cartoons of the period show the rapid deterioration of the regime's image: from the classic figure of the austere Roman matron to that of the Renaissance courtesan. At the turn of the century, a minister of the treasury was accused of ordering the reproduction of his lover's likeness as the representation of the republic on a treasury note.

The difficulties of establishing either an old-style republic or a modern republic in Brazil worried the intellectuals of the time, especially the republicans. The central point of the debate was the relationship between the private and the public, the individual and the community. Various thinkers identified the absence of Anglo-Saxon individualism as an explanation of the Brazilian inability to organize a political society. After a rapid disenchantment with the new regime, the republican theorist Alberto Sales stated that Brazilians were very sociable but not undivided—that is, they managed to live together in small groups but were incapable of organizing into a society. According to him, it was precisely the exaltation of the individual that gave the Americans the organizational capacity so admired by Tocqueville. Along the same lines, Sílvio Romero cited a French author, Edmond Demolins, in characterizing Brazilian psychology as communitarian in nature, in contrast to the individualistic psychology of the Anglo-Saxons. The conclusion that Sílvio Romero drew from this distinction was the same as that of Alberto Sales: Brazilians lacked a spirit of initiative and of collective consciousness, and they reflected an excessive dependence on the state, or what Demolins called the predominance of an alimentary politics.[10]

Even a positivist such as Aníbal Falcão formulated the antimony in the same terms. The difference was that Falcão, as a good positivist, placed the affirmative values on the Brazilian side. The Brazilian tradition, or the Iberian tradition in general, emphasized the integrative, participatory, and affective aspects. The Anglo-Saxon tradition was individualistic, selfish, materialistic, and conflict-prone. The future of humanity lay in the former tradition. In politics, according to Falcão, individualism led to dispersion and conflict, whereas the communitarian approach led to an integrative republican dictatorship.[11]

This debate has continued, as shown by the revival of the theme by Richard M. Morse, a severe critic of Anglo-Saxon culture.[12] According to Morse, the Iberian culture, even today, emphasizes integration, incorporation, and the dominance of the whole over the individual. Such a tradition stems from Spain's preference at the beginning of the modern age for the Thomist view of state and society, in which the notion of community and the conception of the state as an instrument for promoting the common good are paramount.

Such a conception, as is easily verified, is close to that of Aníbal Falcão and the orthodox positivists in general. It was not by accident that Comte stated that he was inspired by the Christian tradition of the Middle Ages. The positivists' concrete proposals, not merely their philosophical positions, were directed toward promoting integration, beginning with their basic demand for the incorporation of the proletariat into society. Preferably, they sought this incorporation through a change in mind-set rather than through class conflict; it should be effected, for example, by the rich recognizing their duty to protect the poor. Other concrete proposals were along the same non-confrontational lines: abolition of slavery by the government, defense of the Indians, and opposition to vagrancy laws. Even the republican transition should be done in a gentle manner: the orthodox positivists wanted the emperor to take the initiative by proclaiming himself the republican dictator.

Despite the admirable dedication of the orthodox positivists, their proposals had only a small, ephemeral effect. Their appeal for integration to communitarian values, made under circumstances of extreme social inequality, an intense power struggle, and unbridled financial speculation, fell on deaf ears. Certain proposals, such as those referring to elevating the role of women and the family, were undoubtedly in the established cultural tradition. But the positivists' efforts were basically conservative in nature, in that they reinforced the prevailing patriarchy. At best, the proposal of making the state an agent of the common harmony of social relationships through the republican dictatorship reinforced governmental paternalism. At worst, it carried water for the mill of technocratic bureaucracy, with or without the military. Community, affection, and love become mere words, if not downright deceptions.

The Brazilian difficulty with the two models of freedom, the ancient and the modern, perhaps lay in the absence of an element that was unaccounted for by both models, yet was, in reality, an important part of and perhaps even a premise of their functioning. In order for the ancient republic to work, for its citizens to accept public freedom instead of individual freedom, and in order for the modern republic to work, for its citizens to largely give up their influence on public affairs in favor of individual freedom, the prior existence of a feeling of community and collective identity was required. In the past, belonging to a city harbored this identity; in modern times, belonging to a nation does. One may ask whether Hamilton's republic without patriots could survive without that sentiment, despite all of the institutional apparatus invented by the founding fathers. One could ask whether, in the French case, something of the revolutionary experience, which was a phenomenon that mobilized but also divided society, could have survived without the sentiment of being a nation that was awakened by wars abroad and by the civilizing crusade that the French soldiers believed they were carrying out in Europe. A sense of identity was the foundation of these two models of a republic. In itself, this sense would not be sufficient to build a political community, because it neglected the universal fact of diversity and conflict. There, probably, lay the error of the proposal of orthodox positivism. But without it, the two models would also disintegrate.

During the beginning of the republic in Brazil, no such sentiment existed. There were certainly elements that served as part of a national identity, such as the unity of language, of religion, and even political unity. It is true that the Paraguayan War (1864–70) had produced the first national sentiment; this was limited, however, since slavery imposed complications. Resistance to recruitment was widespread, and many people freed their slaves simply to have them fight in their place. Later, under the republic, Jacobinism attempted to mobilize patriotism in Rio de Janeiro, but this mobilization ultimately led to division rather than to unity. The principal targets of the Jacobin attacks were the Portuguese, who constituted 20 percent of the population. Many businessmen and bankers were Portuguese, but many were also manual laborers and viewed themselves as excluded from the Jacobin republic. A short time later, the anarchist movement explicitly attacked the idea of the fatherland, which they considered a tool of the masters for domination and an instrument to control markets and divide the working class.

The search for a collective identity for the country, for a foundation for building the nation, was a task pursued by the intellectual generation of the First Republic of Brazil (1889–1930). It was a search for a basis for redefining the republic and establishing a republican government that would be more than a caricature of itself. Disenchantment with the 1889 outcome was common. The propagandists and the major participants in the republican movement quickly perceived that they had not found the republic of their dreams. When his brother held the presidency in 1901, Alberto Sales published a virulent attack on the new regime, which he considered corrupt and more despotic than the monarchy. Perhaps the strongest formulation of disenchantment came from Alberto Torres in the second decade of the century: "This state is not a nationality; this country is not a society; these folk are not people. Our men are not citizens."[13]

chapter two

THE PROCLAMATIONS OF
THE REPUBLIC

We sometimes wonder whether history is not, in large part, a novel by historians.

—Tobias Monteiro[1]

Less than a month had passed since the proclamation of the Republic of Brazil on November 15, 1889, when the French chargé d'affaires in Rio de Janeiro, Camille Blondel, noted the attempt by the victors of that day to construct an official version of the facts, directed at history. The attempt, according to Blondel, was to maximize the role of the principal actors and to minimize the role of chance in what had happened.[2] The French diplomat had perceived a phenomenon common to great events: a battle to construct an official version of the facts and the struggle to establish the myth of origin. In the case of the Brazilian republic, this battle was as important as, if not more important than, the proclamation itself, which was an unexpected, rapid, and bloodless event. At stake were the role definitions of the various actors, the claims that each were judged to have on the new regime, and the very nature of that regime.

The fact that the proclamation was a military phenomenon, with few links to the civilian republican movement, means that a study of it cannot, in itself, explain the nature of the new regime. The advent of the Brazilian republic cannot be reduced to a military question and to the insurrection of military units quartered in São Cristóvão. However, it would be incorrect to dismiss the events of November 15 as simple accidents. Although the roots of the republic must be sought further away and in greater depth, the act of its installation possesses unequaled symbolic value. The struggle over its historical definition was hard-fought for this very reason. Deodoro da Fonseca, Benjamin Constant,[3] Quintino Bocaiúva, and Floriano Peixoto—there was no innocence in the fight to delineate the role of each of these individuals. Behind the struggle was the dispute for power and distinct views of the nature of the new republic.

The Proclamation

I do not intend to reconstruct the different versions of the events of November 15, 1889, that were proffered by the participants. It will suffice to observe that supporters of Deodoro, Constant, Bocaiúva, and Peixoto battled about them for a long time. Their disputes sometimes assumed a passionate character and revolved around apparently irrelevant points. Take the example of what might be called the war of the *vivas* (Long live!). Who shouted "*Viva,*" for whom, or at what, at what time? The versions disagree. Did Marshal Deodoro give a *viva* for the emperor upon entering the General Headquarters? Upon leaving it? Did Benjamin Constant give a *viva* for the republic to drown out the *viva* given the emperor by Deodoro? Did the latter censure the *vivas* given for the republic by claiming that they were premature or that they should be left to the public? What is the significance of the famous painting by Henrique Bernardelli (fig. I, gallery), which now has been transformed into the official and sacred version of the proclamation? Was Deodoro, who posed for the painting, giving *vivas* at that moment (when leaving General Headquarters after the deposing of the cabinet) for the emperor or for the republic? Or was he, without *vivas,* ordering a twenty-one-gun salute to the success in deposing the cabinet or to the success of the proclamation? Finally, was there a moment on November 15 when Deodoro actually proclaimed the republic?

If the war of the *vivas* has to do with Deodoro's participation, other disputes deal with Benjamin Constant's role. Everyone recognizes his influence on the military academies (at Praia Vermelha, and the War College, created in 1889 and located in São Cristóvão). There is no doubt about his republican convictions, but serious disagreements exist as to the importance of his actions on November 15. His followers consider him the founder of the republic and hold him responsible for the military's action. In their view, he provided the ideological foundations, persuaded Deodoro, and avoided the possibility that the episode would become a mere revolt in the barracks. Deodoro's followers reply that Constant himself recognized that nothing could have been done without Deodoro, for the old general was the only person in a position to galvanize the troops through the leadership he exercised over them. On this view, Constant was merely a teacher and one who was unknown to most of the soldiers in the barracks. The historical republicans, especially Quintino Bocaiúva, head of the Brazilian Republican Party, and Francisco Glicério, representative of the São Paulo republicans, reiterate Constant's doubts both on the eve of the proclamation and on the 15th itself. According to their testimony, Constant hesitated until the late afternoon of that day. The historical republicans try to preserve the figure of Deodoro, while at the same time emphasizing their own role in light of the marshal's recognized lack of republican conviction and Constant's doubts.

Finally, after Floriano's ascent to power, there was no shortage of those who attributed to him the central role in the events of November 15. Serzedelo Correia is the principal defender of this position.

Floriano's doubtfulness, as pointed out by many, or even his hostility toward the movement, which was denounced at the time by Deodoro's followers, is transformed by Correia into a shrewdness intended to facilitate the success of the revolt. On this view, the fact that the republic was declared peacefully and without bloodshed is owed to Correia, a republican of long standing.

The dispute over Deodoro da Fonseca, Benjamin Constant, Quintino Bocaiúva, and Floriano Peixoto persisted for a long time and can be followed in the articles and editorials in *O Paiz*, Bocaiúva's newspaper, which spoke for republican officialdom. The dance of words to define each man's role continues to the present. The greatest struggle concerns assigning the title of founder, a title vied for by followers of both Deodoro and Constant. Bocaiúva is rarely described as a founder, but he often appears as a patriarch or apostle. There is a greater consensus supporting Floriano, for he came later: he is the consolidator, the savior of the republic. Those who deny Deodoro the label of founder accord him, in recompense, the title of proclaimer. The distribution of roles is humorously commented upon by "Gavroche" (the pseudonym of Arthur Azevedo) in *O Paiz* for November 19, 1895:

> *Portraits*
> The Necromancer, with good manners,
> Tries to satisfy everyone:
> He gives us Benjamin, the founder,
> Deodoro, the proclaimer,
> Floriano, the consolidator,
> Prudente, the peacemaker!
> This is truly flattery!

Gibes, anecdotes, gossip, *petite histoire,* or a simple dispute among participants in the events? If it were only one of these, the dispute would not have outlived the actors involved. The struggle to establish an official version of November 15 and build a republican pantheon became, as usually happens in all movements for political transformation, a conflict over the definition of the new regime. Although initially only a verbal one, the conflict gradually became more explicit in political battles; to consider it extinct over a century after the events occurred would, perhaps, be premature. An analysis of the struggle over the myth of the founder can serve to clarify the nature of this conflict.

Deodoro: The Military Republic

What did Deodorism represent? It was defended primarily by military sectors with no links to republican propaganda. The Deodorists were, above all, the higher-ranking officers who had fought in the Paraguayan War. They were the countless relatives surrounding the marshal, such as his brothers and nephews, one of whom opened the gates of the General Headquarters on November 15.[4] They were the young officers who mobilized the troops of São Cristóvão, the First and Ninth Cavalry Regiments, the Second Artillery Regiment, and the War College. Distinguishing themselves in this group were Captain Mena Barreto (who fainted from shouting so many *vivas* for the republic at Campo de Santana and who awoke the Viscount of Ouro Preto in prison to tell him he was going to be shot); Captain Trajano Cardoso; Lieutenant Sebastião Bandeira; Second Lieutenant Joaquim Inácio Batista Cardoso (who proposed shooting the emperor); Second Lieutenant Manuel Joaquim Machado; and the cadet-sergeant Plácido de Abreu. With the exception of the last-named, these men met immediately after November 15 to establish what they considered the truth about the facts and to combat the forces that were trying, in their view, to distort history for their own benefit.[5] The most vocal in the group were Mena Barreto and Sebastião Bandeira. Years later, as generals, they were still arguing their version of the facts.

To this group, the proclamation was strictly a military, corporative act executed under the inimitable leadership of Deodoro. Civilians had little or no influence. There were a few civilians at Campo de Santana, but they had not even properly organized the *mise-en-scène:* "the republican leaders had not even prepared the scene for the psychological moment," claims Sebastião Bandeira, agreeing with Aristides Lobo in his famous description of how the people witnessed the proclamation.[6] The view of these young non-positivist officers coincided with that of Deodoro himself and the higher-ranking officers who had participated in the Paraguayan War, many of whom later became involved in the Military Question.[7] To this group, the founding of the republic was the final act of the Military Question; it was their definitive solution for eliminating a regime that was, as they saw it, dominated by a college-educated elite hostile to military interests and disrespectful of the soldierly spirit.

The corporative theme was decisive in convincing Deodoro to take part in the movement. His resistance to admitting civilians—mufti, or tailcoats, as he called them—into the conspiracy is well known. He claimed it was strictly a military matter. Also exercising a decisive influence on the unleashing of the movement was the news, invented on November 14 by Major Sólon, that Deodoro and Constant had been arrested, as well as rumors that the troops at São Cristóvão were about to be attacked by the National Guard, the Black Guard (Guarda Negra), and the police. Ouro Preto, the prime minister, had in fact decided to reorganize the National Guard and strengthen the police as a counterweight to the lack of discipline in the army, but the assertions that he planned to reduce the size of the army or even abolish it were certainly false. Deodoro would explode at each of these pieces of information brought by young officers: "I won't allow it! I'll aim artillery; I'll haul the seven ministers to the public square and then hand myself over to the people to judge me!"[8] Even Floriano Peixoto may have been persuaded by corporative reasons to avoid defending the monarchy. His reply to Deodoro, when the latter probed his feelings about the movement, is well known: "If it is against the tailcoats, I have my old rifle." Deodoro also mentions another statement of Floriano's, in which Floriano, fingering a button of his uniform, declaimed: "Seu Manuel, the monarchy is the enemy of this. If it is an overthrow, I'll be ready."[9]

This group had no detailed vision for a republic. It was merely seeking a position of greater prestige and power, to which its members felt the army was entitled after the Paraguayan War. The imperial political elite, despite the many indications of military discontent, would not relinquish its civilian rule or its belief that a dominant civilian authority was necessary. Ouro Preto's stance is indicative of such conviction taken almost to the point of political blindness. Under normal circumstances, the emperor, taking advantage of his personal relationships, would have been a buffer against the military's complaints. But since 1887, his illness from diabetes had robbed him of the capacity to govern. During the Military Question issue in 1887, Pelotas, a general, had already used as an argument to "put the troops in the street" the fact that the emperor no longer had the will to rule.[10] With the emergence of a military esprit de corps and the disappearance of any possibility of maintaining the privileged relationship between the leaders and the emperor, the military had to deal directly with the cabinet and parliament—that is, with the civilian political elite, which had always prided itself on having kept Brazil away from the caudillismo, regarded as a sign of political barbarism, that dominated Brazil's neighboring republics. On November 16, on receiving the messenger from Saraiva, the newly appointed president of the Council of Ministers, Deodoro answered that it was too late, that the republic had been proclaimed and that Ouro Preto and Count d'Eu were to blame, the latter for not using his influence to prevent the ministers from oppressing the military.[11] The group's position is summarized in Deodoro's phrase to Ilha Moreira on the eve of the movement: the republic is the army's salvation.[12]

Deodorism clearly appears in the well-known painting by Bernardelli that depicts the proclamation of the republic. (See again fig. I.) The work is dominated by the equestrian figure of the marshal, which occupies the entire foreground. The other figures appear in the background and in secondary postures: Benjamin Constant and Quintino Bocaiúva are on the same plane and both are on horseback; Aristides Lobo is on foot. The painting's style is that of the classical exaltation of the military hero, who is raised above common mortals by sitting astride a spirited mount. It is the exaltation of the victorious, great man, the maker of history. The personalistic emphasis is even stronger here than in the canvas of the proclamation of independence by Pedro Américo. Américo's painting depicts the figure of Pedro I interacting with several others. This reflection of collective action is absent from Bernardelli's image, perhaps because there was less need to affirm the role of the first emperor in events. The only element missing from Bernardelli's work is the sword, a symbol of military action. Most likely, its absence was because Deodoro carried no sword on November 15, despite statements to the contrary. To represent him raising his gleaming sword, as Major Jacques Ourique wished, would have been too great a violation of the truth. As it was, the meaning of the gesture of raising his cap created doubt.

Benjamin Constant: The Sociocratic Republic

Defenders of the primacy of Benjamin Constant in the proclamation represent a very distinct political and ideological group. The difference already appears in the terms with which Constant was described or deified. Alongside the classification of him as founder—in direct dispute with Deodoro—appeared other words that better described his attributed role. He was the catechist, the apostle, the evangelist, the indoctrinator, the thinker, the master, and the idol of the younger military. Constant does not primarily appear as a representative of the military class, as an avenger, or as the savior of the army. Instead, he appears as the teacher, the theoretician, and the bearer of a view of history and a plan for Brazil. That the events of November 15 went beyond a mere barracks revolt aimed at overthrowing the Ouro Preto cabinet, to become a regime change, a revolution, and the salvation of the country, was said to be Constant's deed.

Orthodox positivists offered the most elaborate version of this view. Constant had clashed with Miguel Lemos and left the Positivist Society in 1882, although he maintained a cordial relationship with its orthodox leaders. Immediately after the proclamation, on November 17, they pursued close contact with him, which was maintained until his death in 1891. In his biography of Constant, published in 1892, Teixeira Mendes placed Constant alongside Tiradentes and José Bonifácio in the Brazilian civic pantheon. Tiradentes for the Inconfidência, José Bonifácio for independence, and Constant for the republic—for the orthodox republicans, this was the civic trinity that symbolized the march of Brazilian society toward its historical destiny, which, during its positivist phase, was also the culmination of humanity.[13]

Beyond any doubt, Constant and his followers also manipulated the corporative element. The glorification of the students at the Military School and the War College reflected corporative and anti-civilian characteristics. The restoration of military dignity was incessantly mentioned. For Constant, however, the army was more an instrument of action than its end. Perhaps this was the basis for his hesitation on November 15. As a positivist, although not an orthodox one, there was nothing of the militarist about him; he was repulsed by the idea of force dominating politics. A pacifist, he dreamed of seeing an end to armies and a relegation of all weapons to museums. Ironically, he was using the army to achieve a social state that rejected the army. At the time, Sílvio Romero pointed out this incongruity. Militarism and positivism were, in his words, two things that "hurlent de se trouver ensemble" (howl at finding themselves together). The orthodox positivists informed Constant of their disapproval of the republic's manner of conception. In their opinion, the imperial elite, led by the emperor, should have carried out the transition. But this conviction did not prevent Teixeira Mendes from exhorting republicans on that same day, November 15: "Proclaim the dictatorship! Proclaim the dictatorship!" Nor did it eliminate the fact that behind support for Constant lay an elaborate vision of the republic.[14]

Such a vision conflicted not only with Deodorism but also, and especially, with the position of a good number of the historical republicans. The division between democratic and sociocratic currents was debated; democracy was understood as the position of the non-positivist historical republicans, who advocated an American-style representative republic or perhaps one like the French Third Republic. The sociocrats, or positivists, were avowed enemies of representative democracy, which to them characterized the metaphysical state of mankind. They believed that it should be replaced with a republican dictatorship, a form of government inspired as much by the classical Roman tradition as by the figure of Georges Danton at the time of the Committee of Public Safety during the French Revolution. Under this model, the congress would have a mere budgetary role. The republican dictator would govern for life and choose his successor. The dictatorship's goal was to promote the social republic, that is, to guarantee all spiritual freedoms and to promote the incorporation of the proletariat into society by eliminating the privileges of the bourgeoisie.

In its pure form, the school linked to Constant remained confined to the proposals of the orthodox positivists and found no practical application. But it did contribute to various measures during the early years of the Brazilian republic, especially to the separation of church and state, the introduction of civil marriage, the secularization of cemeteries, the beginning of contact with the working class, and the reform of military instruction. The idea of a dictatorial, social, and virtuous republic, as well as an opposition to political representation and to the college-educated elite, partially fused this school with the Jacobinism that emerged during Floriano's administration and that characterized republican policy until 1897. Although Floriano was Catholic and hated positivism, the style of government that he represented—authoritarian, opposed to the educated elite, opposed to large capital, moralistic (at least in appearance), and populist—shared several points with the positivist proposal, despite that doctrine's opposition to militarism.

If the republic of the Deodorists ultimately sought to save the army, the republic of the school of Benjamin Constant wanted to save the country. The latter absorbed from positivism an integrated view of history, an interpretation of past and present, and a projection of the future. Further, it incorporated a messianic tendency, or a conviction in the missionary role of both military and civilian positivists. History had its laws and its predetermined movement in well-defined phases, but human action, and especially that of great men, could hasten mankind's evolutionary march. That march, in Brazil's case, proceeded through the establishment of a republic that would

guarantee the material order, which was understood as the incorporation of the proletariat into society, and spiritual freedom—that is,
it would end the monopoly of the church and the state in education,
religion, and science.

The civilian orthodox positivists planned to achieve all this
through those who possessed a technical training: doctors, engineers,
mathematicians. Thus composed, the dauntless vanguard could, in
their view, effect the great transformation. It was a kind of middle-
class bolshevism, which will be discussed later. Many positivists,
however, were not resigned to the exclusive use of persuasion as a
tactic. They became involved in the political struggle, in conspiracies
and revolts, despite facing disapproval and even excommunication
from the positivist Apostolate.[15] Such was the case for Silva Jardim,
Benjamin Constant, and others. Military positivism encountered the
same fate, especially in the military academies, which entered a state
of almost perpetual political agitation that was interrupted only in
1904, at the time of the Vaccine Revolt in Rio de Janeiro. Civilian
Jacobinism, which evolved around the figure of Floriano, also did
not limit itself to the restrictions of the orthodox positivists.[16]

The positivist movement left its mark, as evidenced by various
republican monuments dedicated to the following figures: Benjamin
Constant, located in Republic Square in Rio de Janeiro; Floriano, in
Rio de Janeiro's Cinelândia section; and Júlio de Castilhos, in Porto
Alegre. All are works of the positivist artists Eduardo de Sá and
Décio Villares. Similar in conception, the three monuments constitute veritable political discourses. They obey not only Comte's political and philosophical ideas but also his aesthetic conceptions, by
which art should idealize reality, exalt the altruistic, affective side of
the human being, and promote the civic worship of the family, the
country, and humanity. According to the orientation of the positivist
Apostolate, civic worship in Brazil included the figures of Tiradentes, José Bonifácio, and Benjamin Constant, in addition to the republican flag designed by Décio Villares.

The monument to Benjamin Constant, executed by Décio Villares and inaugurated in 1925, was proposed and conceived by Teixeira Mendes as early as 1892. According to Teixeira Mendes, there

5. Décio Villares, Monument to Benjamin Constant,
Rio de Janeiro.

6. Eduardo de Sá, Monument to Floriano Peixoto,
Rio de Janeiro.

7. Monument to Floriano Peixoto,
detail.

was no doubt that Constant should be depicted in the action of November 15, but it was necessary to clarify that he acted "sustained morally by the Family and driven by the *Patria,* in the service of Humanity." The symbolic figure of the republic, represented by a woman, should dominate the monument. Constant should appear with the republican flag across his chest, prominently displaying the phrase "Order and Progress." Bas-reliefs would represent scenes from the hero's life.[17] Décio Villares's work followed nearly all of Teixeira Mendes's recommendations. The only significant modification, which does not depart from positivist symbolism, was the replacement of the *Patria* at the top of the monument by Humanity, also represented by a woman, but now with a child against her bosom. Constant, with the flag behind him, is turned to face the General Headquarters. In the medallions and bas-reliefs on the four sides of the monument appear scenes from his life, including the crucial moment of November 15, where Constant is depicted at Deodoro's side on an equal footing, thus offering a certain counterpoint to the figure of the marshal; while the latter is raising his cap, Constant keeps his lowered. The figures of Tiradentes and José Bonifácio also appear in the medallions. In one of the bas-reliefs, on the opposite side, the figure of Danton references the French Revolution. In one of the more daring medallions, Christopher Columbus presides over a ceremony in which Benjamin Constant returns the trophies of the Paraguayan War to Paraguayan President Francia. The bronze used for the monument came from melting down two cannons, one Brazilian, the other Paraguayan. Everywhere on the monument are reproductions of positivist slogans and Benjamin Constant's phrases, such as "My religion is the religion of Humanity."

A similar vision imbues the monument to Floriano Peixoto, a work by Eduardo de Sá. The work was inaugurated in 1910, but an announcement of the project dates from 1901. In a composition entitled *Guarding the Flag,* Floriano's figure stands atop a pedestal. As in the previous monument, the republican flag forms a backdrop to the statue. In its bas-relief are the heads of Tiradentes and José Bonifácio and the bust of Benjamin Constant. To the left, the figure of a young woman extends her right hand, blessing the past and pointing toward the future of the fatherland. The base of the monument is shaped like a civic altar, referencing the altars erected in Paris after the Revolution of 1789. In the altar's niches are four groups in bronze and a statue. The four groups represent the three races that make up the Brazilian population, and the Catholic religion, by means of reference to four famous poems of Brazilian literature: "Caramuru" (the white race), "The Waterfall of Paulo Afonso" (the black race), "Y Juca-Pirama" (the yellow race), and "Anchieta" (Catholicism).[18] The statue, a figure of a woman holding a rose, is intended to signify the mixed race suggested by the fusion of the three ethnicities and the predominance of feeling and love. Panels in bas-relief show Floriano's collaborators. There were so many figures that, according to Francisco de Assis Barbosa, it was said at the time that Floriano, at the top of the monument, seemed to be shouting: "No one else is coming up here!"[19]

8. Décio Villares, Monument to Júlio de Castilhos,
Porto Alegre.

9. Monument to Júlio de Castilhos,
detail.

The monument provoked widespread controversy. There were complaints about its sectarian nature and that it represented the attempt of one school of thought, one political faction, to take undue control of a figure who belonged to all republicans. The polemic was prolonged by the fact that Floriano, unlike Benjamin Constant and Júlio de Castilhos, was not a positivist. In reality, the monument was an effort by positivists to appropriate his memory. It is not without significance that Floriano was placed on the monument guarding the republican flag conceived by the positivists. It is known that Floriano disliked the flag and, as president, even encouraged a bill that would have modified it by removing the positivist motto. This will be discussed later.[20]

The concept for the monument to Júlio de Castilhos, which was inaugurated in 1913 in Porto Alegre, hardly differs from those described above. The work is by the same Décio Villares who executed the statue of Benjamin Constant, and it consists of a pyramid at whose top stands the figure of the Republic of Brazil in the form of a woman. At her feet lies a globe with twenty-one stars representing the Federation and the inevitable "Order and Progress." At the base of the pyramid, on four sides, appear various scenes from the life of Júlio de Castilhos, along with the traditional references to Tiradentes, José Bonifácio, and the French Revolution. Positivist mottos are distributed throughout the monument.[21]

Quintino Bocaiúva: The Liberal Republic

In 1889, Quintino Bocaiúva represented the republican propaganda that began, somewhat ostentatiously, with the Manifesto of 1870, a document to which he had greatly contributed. In May 1889, during the Federal Republican Convention held in São Paulo, Bocaiúva was elected head of the Brazilian Republican Party. This position allowed him to speak for republicans from São Paulo as well as other provinces. Despite divergences within the party regarding which methods to employ for regime change, he represented all the civic propagandists on November 15.

Defending his role, however, was more problematic than defending his participation in both military factions, simply because November 15 was decided upon and effected by the military. Civilian republicans were notified of the conspiracy only four days prior to its execution. Even so, as we have observed, this involvement of civilians was contrary to Deodoro's will. However, to ensure its legitimacy, it was important that the movement not resemble a simple military action. The presence of historical republicans was fundamental to the event, since it would dismiss the irony of a proclamation that was alien to their lengthy and developed efforts.

The alliance with the military to establish a republic was discussed among the propagandists. It was Bocaiúva who defended such an alternative. He himself confessed that he was disinclined to go into the streets without the "yellow button": "Without the armed forces at our side, any agitation in the streets would be not only an act of folly . . . but an especially certain, predictable defeat."[22] For this, he was called a militarist in republican circles. Another person who accepted collaboration with the military was Francisco Glicério, whom Campos Sales sent to Rio de Janeiro upon being advised by Aristides Lobo of the conspirators' plans. Some disagreed with this alternative either because they defended the establishment of a republic by revolutionary means or by popular revolt, as was the case for Silva Jardim, or because they desired a peaceful revolution, as did Américo Brasiliense, Bernardino de Campos, Saldanha Marinho, and perhaps the majority of São Paulo republicans. It is symptomatic of this fact that neither Silva Jardim nor Saldanha Marinho was alerted to the conspiracy.

One of the great problems for the historical republicans was the party's situation in Rio de Janeiro. Its traditional and highly respected leader, Saldanha Marinho, could not control it given the divisions among its various factions—evolutionists, revolutionaries, civilists, militarists. The republicans from São Paulo were restive about the situation in Rio de Janeiro. In 1887, Campos Sales wrote to Saldanha Marinho that "the delay in the republican idea in Brazil is due almost completely to the lack of good organization in the capital city of the Empire."[23] At the end of 1888 and the beginning of 1889, the Rio party was in a crisis. Saldanha wrote to the São Paulo republicans and threatened to resign. According to him, there was merely the semblance of a party in Rio de Janeiro. Controlling it, he added, "was a task beyond the *powers of anyone*."[24] The discouragement with respect to taking effective action, as shown by the republican group in Rio de Janeiro, was also shared by the radicals in the group. At the party convention held in 1888, Barata Ribeiro, the future Florianist city mayor, displayed his skepticism by stating that it was from the provinces that they should expect the movement's victory. At most, Rio de Janeiro could contribute pyrotechnics.[25]

Deodorists asked republicans for such pyrotechnics on November 15. According to Lieutenant Bandeira, even these were poorly organized, a view corroborated by the historical republican Aristides Lobo. This version of events was quite uncomfortable to the civilians and even to militarists such as Bocaiúva. The military presence was undeniable, but it was necessary to transform it into a mere instrument that served the designs of the historical republican wing. Deodoro's position was sympathetic to that wing precisely because it was corporative. Deodoro represented the support of the military, without interfering in the conception of the new regime or even in its functioning. To the historical republicans, it was sufficient to emphasize the marshal's hesitations at the meeting on November 11 and after the overthrow of the cabinet of Ouro Preto. In the group's version of these events, Bocaiúva appeared both times as the person who persuaded Deodoro to favor the republic. On the 15th, Bocaiúva also supposedly persuaded Major Sólon to tell Deodoro that he would not return his sword to its scabbard until the republic was unequivocally and definitively proclaimed.

More important than stating the position of the historical republicans vis-à-vis Deodoro was stating it vis-à-vis Benjamin Constant. If the glorification of Deodoro was compatible with the proposal of the historical republicans, or at least a portion of them, then the glorification of Constant was not, for he represented not only military interference but also a conflicting idea of the republic and a determination to define the paths of the new regime. The paths of Constant were positivist paths. If there were positivists among historical republicans, especially in Rio Grande do Sul, they were not in the majority in Rio de Janeiro, much less in São Paulo, where the movement's greatest strength lay. The sociocratic republic of the positivists was incompatible with the democratic republic of the São Paulo republicans, that is, with the representative republic modeled on North America. To the positivists, the latter was a metaphysical regime, a parliamentary dictatorship, and a "bourgeois-ocracy." The great ideological adversaries of the historical republicans were the positivists, not the Deodorists.

It is not surprising, then, that Quintino Bocaiúva's and Francisco Glicério's version of the republic sought to reduce Constant's role more than Deodoro's. It depicted Constant as ingenuous and a victim of "natural and constant indecision." Instead of the leader offered by positivists as the antidote to Deodoro's hesitations and the one who, at decisive moments such as those of November 11 and 15, guaranteed that the movement was no mere barracks revolt, there appears a Constant who is nearly as hesitant as Deodoro, if not more so. Constant, who was faced with the increasingly serious state of the marshal's health on November 14, is described as showing complete discouragement; on this version, he proposed postponing the movement or virtually resigned himself to its failure, and he showed concern about the consequences of the reprisals that were certain to fall on the military.[26]

According to Bocaiúva, it was his decision, supported by Sólon, to fabricate inflammatory rumors of the movement of troops from the São Cristóvão regiments and thus define the situation that led to the proclamation. He even claims that the republic was established on the 14th, at 6 p.m., in São Francisco square, during his meeting with Sólon. His decision, the boldness of Sólon, and the heroism of Deodoro were, according to him, the ingredients that made the new republic. The decision was that of the historical republicans and of the leader of the Republican Party; the military was the instrument that freely agreed to implement it. Bocaiúva suggests that the Military Question itself was part of republican tactics to agitate the barracks against the government. And Sena Madureira, "our comrade," had initiated the conflict with this in mind.

There is more. According to the historical republicans, Constant's hesitation increased after the overthrow of the cabinet. By the end of the afternoon on November 15, there was still no formal proclamation of the republic by the movement's military leadership. The demonstration by the Municipal Chamber, led by José do Patrocínio, requested exactly that: a unequivocal decree of the new regime. In response to a committee that went to Deodoro's home to demand such a measure, Constant had answered from the window (Deodoro was bedridden, suffering from another attack of dyspnea) that a new regime could not be imposed on the country, and that it was necessary to consult the population by means of a plebiscite. This caused Captain Mário Hermes da Fonseca, one of Deodoro's nephews and a direct participant in the events, to refer to Constant as "the plebiscite man."[27]

The affirmation of the role of the historical republicans was therefore important to guarantee the position of the civilians in the proclamation and the liberal perspective of the republic. But it was impossible to deny the military aspect of the event and the unexpected nature of its emergence. Every newspaper in Rio registered these two elements. One compiler of the news published in the first days of the republic recognized "the unanimous feeling of surprise produced by the establishment of the republican form in Brazil."[28] Arthur Azevedo, an unsuspecting republican, said that Aristides Lobo's expression—stupefied (*bestializado*)—had a cruel appropriateness to it, for "the people of Rio look at each other in astonishment, questioning with their eyes without saying a word." As he returned home at two o'clock in the morning, everything was calm and deserted in the Rocio (today, Tiradentes Square). Four street cleaners were singing as they swept Rua Espírito Santo. When he saw them, the dramatist thought: "These men didn't know, perhaps, that there had been a revolution that day."[29]

The military nature of the operation was also much too evident to be denied. What the people in the city saw was, as Aristides Lobo put it, a military parade led by Deodoro. After the overthrow of the cabinet in Campo de Santana, the parade continued down Rua da Constituição, passing through the Rocio and on to Rua do Teatro; through the Largo de São Francisco, down Rua Ouvidor and Primeiro de Março, to the Naval Arsenal and the Rua Larga de São Joaquim (today Marechal Floriano), from which it returned to the São Cristóvão barracks. En route, the parade was accompanied by groups of the people, harangued by Lopes Trovão and José do Patrocínio on Rua Ouvidor. According to Arthur Azevedo, the cortege proceeded along Primeiro de Março in deep silence. Deodoro looked like a defeated hero, barely remaining upright in the saddle, his expression sullen and his face a color between rust and green.[30]

In the Constituent Assembly, there were frequent debates about the military nature of the proclamation. Some civilians, such as Costa Júnior, complained about the nearly daily statements that the proclamation was owed exclusively to the military, an interpretation that he considered demoralizing for the national character. The military members of the Assembly, such as Major Espírito Santo, were not the only ones who affirmed the supremacy of their class in the events. Historical republicans who were uninvolved in the creation of a "less demoralizing" version of events openly admitted the fact. This was the case for the outspoken Martinho Prado Júnior, who openly stated that "the military made the republic" and criticized the civilians for submitting to the plans of the barracks. Military interference, according to him, had made the proclamation of a republic possible at a time when the republicans were an insignificant part of the population. As a result, the difference between the old regime and the new was hardly discernible. It was not the republic of his dreams.[31]

In such circumstances, it was difficult, if not impossible, to elaborate a myth of origin based on civilian predominance. How could one construct a monument to the proclamation presenting Bocaiúva, Glicério, or Aristides Lobo as the main figures? Even within the positivist aesthetic, in which idealization was the rule, such an effort lacked even minimal credibility. On November 15, the republicans appeared in the background as supporting actors or extras in charge of the pyrotechnics. Their moment of greatest visibility was the brief and rather tumultuous scene at the Municipal Chamber. Despite this and the ceremony that failed to decisively resolve the situation, their hero was unconvincing. Patrocínio, the alderman who promoted the action, had only recently violently criticized the republicans and was hated by them for his connections to the Black Guard. Besides displaying the wrong hero, the ceremony also exhibited the wrong symbol. The flag that Patrocínio raised in the Chamber building was that of the Lopes Trovão Republican Club, an imitation of the American banner, which four days later was replaced by what had become the official positivist version.

Just as no civilian republican leader made any gesture that could be immortalized in art, the Brazilian people were also far from reflecting the role of the populace in the French Revolution. Despite his efforts, not even Silva Jardim himself was allowed onstage on the 15th. The people remained curious about events, asking one another about what was going on, responding to shouts of *viva!*, and following the military parade through the streets. There was no storming of the Bastille or march on Versailles, and there were no acts of heroism. The people were not in the proclamation's script, whether military or civilian, or whether by Deodoro, Constant, or Bocaiúva. The sole example of popular initiative occurred at the end of the military parade, when the army troops left the Naval Arsenal to return to their barracks. The spectators accompanying the parade asked Lopes Trovão to buy them a drink. A bill for forty mil-réis ended up being footed by the tavern owner, for Lopes Trovão had only eleven mil-réis in his pocket. This anonymous merchant unwittingly became the greatest symbol of the people in the new regime: the one who pays the bill.[32]

The attempts to construct the myth of origin of the republic reveal the contradictions that marked the beginning of the regime, even among those who promoted it—contradictions that would not disappear with the passage of time. Divisions among the military factions were long-lived. It is not unreasonable, for example, to see in both the Lieutenants' Movement, begun in 1922, and the nationalist agitation led by the Military Club, in the 1950s, an explicit resonance of the positivist approach. In 1930 there was open talk of establishing a republican dictatorship. In the decade of the 1950s, there were frequent references to Benjamin Constant and to the intense political involvement of the military that had characterized the end of the Brazilian empire and the beginning of the republic. There were even military men who were remnants of orthodox positivism, such as the generals Horta Barbosa and Cândido Rondon.

Among the military, however, there was a great effort to eliminate division. Deodorism was reinforced by the professionalism of officers trained in Germany and by the French Mission. In the 1930s, this professionalism was placed at the service of political intervention through the actions of Góes Monteiro. Góes Monteiro's criticism of the influence of positivism in the army is well known. He considered it a factor that corroded professional spirit and training. The Estado Novo (New State) in the late 1930s took the battle for unity to the symbolic level. Benjamin Constant's statue was moved from its central position in Republic Square, facing the General Headquarters, to one hidden amid the trees in the square. But, as a sign of the times, neither Deodoro nor Floriano took Constant's place. The new military plan needed a nondivisive figure, a symbol not only of military unity but of the unity of the nation itself. The candidate had to be found in the empire: the duke of Caxias. He came to represent the conservative national face of the republic.[33]

Although the military succeeded in eliminating a good part of its differences, divisions remained among civilians and between civilians and the military. One of the reasons for the failure of the 1989 centennial celebrations of the republic may lie precisely in the embarrassment that they caused after twenty years of military rule. For civilians, coming out of the long struggle to demilitarize the republic, it was difficult to once again speak of the generals who had established it and who considered it their property. For the military as an institution, it was not in its interest to rehash the differences that marked the earliest moments of the regime, which included conflicts not only within the army but also between the army and navy.[34]

The myth of origin remained inconclusive, as inconclusive as the republic itself.

chapter three

TIRADENTES

A Hero for the Republic

The struggle over the myth of origin of the republic demonstrates the difficulty in constructing a hero for the new regime. Heroes are powerful symbols, embodiments of ideas and aspirations, points of reference, and fulcrums of collective identification. They are therefore effective in reaching the citizenry's hearts and minds and in legitimizing political regimes. There is no regime that does not promote the worship of its heroes or that prevails without creating its own civic pantheon. For some regimes, heroes emerge almost spontaneously from the struggles preceding the new order. For others, of less popular depth, the promotion of a heroic figure requires effort. In these latter cases, the hero is particularly important. Lacking true popular involvement in their founding, these regimes attempt to compensate through symbolic mobilization. But because the creation of symbols is not arbitrary and does not take place in a social vacuum, it becomes one of the greatest difficulties in constructing a civic pantheon. Any self-respecting hero must bear the face of the nation. He must answer to some collective need or aspiration and reflect some kind of personality or behavior that corresponds to a collectively valued model. If such qualities are absent, any efforts to mythify political figures will be futile. At best, the majority will ignore these would-be heroes; at worst, it will ridicule them.

Some Brazilian citizens went to great lengths to transform the main participants in the events of November 15, 1889, into heroes of the new regime. Poetry and prose in books and newspapers, civic demonstrations, monuments, paintings, and laws of the republic all proclaimed their virtues. Institutions, streets and squares in cities, and warships bore their names. Paintings such as Bernardelli's *The Proclamation of the Republic,* exalting Deodoro da Fonseca, were created for public admiration.

Deodoro was the most obvious candidate for the role of the republican hero, not only because of his undisputed leadership of the military movement that overthrew the monarchy, but also because of his actions on November 15. The aging soldier, moribund just a day before; struggling to stay in the saddle; placing himself at the head of his troops and courageously entering the General Headquarters: here was the stuff of heroism. But powerful factors such as his uncertain republicanism, his bearing as a general under the monarchy, and his physical appearance, which recalled that of another illustrious elder, namely, the emperor, militated against Deodoro, as evidenced on November 15 itself. He was too closely linked to the military to win broad public support. In the struggles involving the beginning of the republic, Deodoro, identified with the army, divided as much as he united.

Another candidate vying for the role of republican hero was Benjamin Constant. His republicanism was beyond reproach, but he did not look like a hero. He was neither a military nor a popular leader. In Eduardo Prado's cruel characterization, he was a bloodless general and an unpublished sage, exhibiting "a blank book under his virgin sword."[1] However much the positivists, the ingenious manipulators of symbols, attempted to promote him as one of the components of the Brazilian civic trinity, alongside Tiradentes and José Bonifácio, his appeal was more limited than Deodoro's. Within the army, he appealed only to the youth, to students in the military academies and to younger officers; in the civilian milieu, he attracted, almost exclusively, positivists.

THE FORMATION
OF SOULS

Gallery

I. Henrique Bernardelli, *The Proclamation of the Republic*,
Military Academy at Agulhas Negras

II. Aurélio de Figueiredo,
The Martyrdom of Tiradentes,
National Historical Museum

III. Décio Villares,
Tiradentes,
Mariano Procópio Museum

IV. Pedro Américo, *Tiradentes Quartered,*
Mariano Procópio Museum

V. Eduardo de Sá, *The Reading of the Sentence*,
National Historical Museum

VI. José Walsht Rodrigues,
Second Lieutenant Joaquim José da Silva Xavier,
National Historical Museum

VII. Eugène Delacroix, *Liberty Leading the People*,
The Louvre

VIII. *O Malho*, Untitled,
November 26, 1904

IX. Décio Villares, *Republic*,
Museum of the Republic

X. Décio Villares, *Banner of Humanity,*
Positivist Church of Brazil

XI. Belmiro de Almeida, *Dame à la rose*,
National Museum of Fine Arts

XII. Pedro Américo, *The Carioca Woman*,
National Museum of Fine Arts

XIII. Flag of the Empire, National Historical Museum

XIV. Flag of the Lopes Trovão Republican Club,
Historical Museum of the City of Rio de Janeiro

XV. Flag raised in Alagoas, Museum of the Republic

XVI. Flag designed by Décio Villares, Positivist Church of Brazil

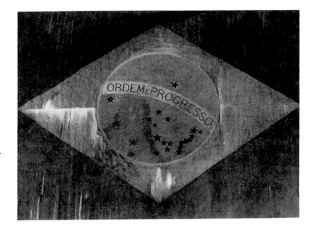

XVII. Flag sewn by the daughters of Benjamin Constant, Positivist Church of Brazil

XVIII. Pedro Bruno, *The Fatherland*, Museum of the Republic

XIX. Clotilde de Vaux

A more serious candidate for the role was Floriano Peixoto. Un-distinguished at first and distrusted by both monarchists and repub-licans, he acquired greater dimensions following the Naval Revolt in Rio de Janeiro and the Federalist Revolt in southern Brazil. His re-sistance to the uprisings inspired the republican Jacobins in Rio de Janeiro, a movement that for the first time gave the republic a popu-lar tinge. To the Jacobins, civilian and military alike, he was beyond doubt the republican hero par excellence. The strength of his appeal, at least in Rio de Janeiro, left traces in popular memory.[2] But if he did not divide civilians from soldiers, nevertheless he created divi-sions within the armed forces (army against navy) and between civil-ians (Jacobins against liberals). The same qualities that were exalted by Jacobins—his republican purity and bravery—were branded as bloody and despotic by liberal republicans. Floriano was possibly the hero of one type of republic, the Jacobin, but he was not the hero of the gradually forming, subsequent type of republic.

Thus, efforts to promote these candidates to the status of hero were largely fruitless. The brief, historical resonance of November 15 (a military parade) did not offer adequate ground for the creation of myths. The number of dedicated republicans was small; popular par-ticipation was almost nonexistent; and events took place in the slip-pery space between the heroic and the comical.[3] The potential heroes also lacked the historical depth and stature demanded by the role. They did not belong to the republican propaganda movement, which had been active since 1870. They were not even recognized as mili-tary heroes. Their participation in the Paraguayan War was little known before the advent of the republic. The recognized heroes of the war were Caxias, Osório, and Tamandaré. The elevation of Deo-doro and Floriano to war heroes occurred after their participation in the proclamation of the republic and was part of the process of the efforts to turn them into myths.

The search for a hero for the republic finally found success in a place that many of the participants in the proclamation of the new republic would never have imagined. In the face of the difficulty of promoting the protagonists of November 15, Tiradentes gradually fulfilled the demands of a mythic hero.[4] Tiradentes was not unknown to the republicans. Campos Sales kept a portrait of Tiradentes in his office. The republican clubs in Rio de Janeiro and Minas Gerais, and those of a lesser scale in the provinces, had tried to resurrect his memory, beginning in the 1870s. As early as 1867, Saldanha Marinho, president of the province of Minas Gerais and future leader of the Republican Party in Rio, had a monument to Tiradentes erected in Ouro Preto. The date of his execution, April 21, 1792, was first celebrated in 1881 in Rio de Janeiro. Even in the faraway province of Rio Grande do Sul, which had many of its own candidates for the hero of the republic, a newspaper in Pelotas submitted a proposal in 1881 for a monument honoring Tiradentes.[5] But the leaders of these clubs did not occupy center stage on November 15. The president of the Tiradentes Club of Rio de Janeiro, Sampaio Ferraz, learned of the plans for the revolt, but he played a secondary role in it. Sampaio Ferraz later encountered problems in paying homage to Tiradentes even during the Floriano period. What, then, were the reasons for adopting Tiradentes, and what was so heroic about him?

An intense historiographic debate about Tiradentes existed then and continues up to the present. (His name literally means "toothpuller.") Even today, his true role in the Inconfidência uprising, his personality and convictions, and his physical appearance are disputed. These discussions do not pertain to the matter at hand. I do not intend to enter the debate about whether Tiradentes was a leader or merely a follower, whether he was a revolutionary or simply a talker, whether he was rich or poor, white or mulatto, or likable or sullen-looking. These debates interest me only insofar as they illuminate the construction of the myth. Assuredly, the preoccupation with the construction of the myth affects and conditions the historiographic debate. Yet in this case, it also transcends that debate and develops within an area of reasoning that surpasses the limits and canons of the historiography. The domain of myth is the collective imagination manifested in the written and oral tradition, in artistic production, and in rituals. A myth can develop despite documentary evidence; the collective imagination can interpret evidence according to symbolic mechanisms that do not necessarily mesh with the historical narrative.

Little is known about the memory of Tiradentes among the people of Minas Gerais and Rio de Janeiro. Such memory should exist, since several documents of the period testify to a great commotion among the population of the *capitania*[6] of Minas Gerais and the city of Rio, caused by the trial of the men accused of the Inconfidência uprising and especially by the execution of Tiradentes. The anonymous author of *Memória do êxito que teve a conjuração de Minas* (Memoir of the Success of the Conspiracy of Minas Gerais), for example, was an eyewitness to the events in Rio de Janeiro and constantly refers to the great dismay of the city's inhabitants. The author, obliged to praise the queen and her justice, personified the city to express his personal feelings. "The city," he writes, had never seen such a dreadful, ugly, and pompous execution. The news of the death penalty for the eleven prisoners, announced on April 19, 1792, shook "the city," which, "without dissenting from its political duties (read: the duty of rendering loyalty to the queen) could not completely hide the oppression it felt." Many families withdrew to the countryside, the streets were deserted, and "consternation seemed to be painted on every object." The announcement of the pardon of all of the prisoners except Tiradentes had the opposite effect, although one no less powerful: "the city felt instant relief from the unaccustomed weight that bore down on it"; the streets were jammed; people came to their windows, and "many, many could not hold back their tears."[7]

Friar Raimundo de Penaforte, the confessor of the participants in the Inconfidência, relates the "inexpressible outpouring of the people" to witness the execution. "The people were innumerable," he insists; if not for the military patrols, he would have been crushed under its immense mass. Such an outpouring of people possibly resulted from the curiosity created by the spectacle of a hanging. But Penaforte, a witness above reproach since he was a docile instrument of the queen's justice, leaves no doubt about the crowd's motivation: "Such was the compassion of the people over the temporal misfortune of the prisoner that to hasten his eternal life they voluntarily offered alms to say masses for his soul."[8]

There is also the account that Joaquim Silvério dos Reis, the traitor among the plotters, was unable to live in peace in Rio de

Janeiro, his place of residence following his rejection by the people of Minas Gerais. The popular animosity was so great that he changed his name by adding Montenegro and moved to Maranhão. People wouldn't speak to him; when they did, it was to hurl insults. If we hold his account as true, he also faced an attempt on his life with a firearm, and his house was set on fire.[9]

It is unreasonable to suppose that the imprisonment of so many important people, the judicial investigation, and the exhibiting of Tiradentes's head in the main square of Vila Rica failed to make a deep and lasting impression on people in Minas Gerais. And it was not merely a matter of Vila Rica. The conspiracy involved important individuals from São João del Rei (chosen for the capital of the republic), Mariana, Tejuco, and Borda do Campo. Documents from the time state that "desolation spread through the *capitania*" after the arrest of the conspirators.[10] When he visited the province in the midnineteenth century, Richard Burton noted that the memory of those events was kept alive and that the population found the punishment imposed on the conspirators excessive and unjust.[11]

It should be remembered that several of the plotters returned from exile. Two of them took part in the Constituent Assembly of 1823: José de Resende Costa, Jr., and the priest Manuel Rodrigues da Costa. Resende Costa, Jr., died in 1841 during the Second Reign,[12] but not before translating and annotating, at the behest of the Historical and Geographical Institute, the chapter from Robert Southey's *History of Brazil* on the Inconfidência. Manuel Rodrigues made an appeal to the central government in favor of those involved in the Minas Gerais uprising of 1842. The participant and historian of that movement, Father José Antônio Marinho, clearly referred to the Inconfidência when he wrote, "the province of Minas has the glory of having given the first martyrs to the independence and liberty of Brazil in the last century."[13] Also note that Maria Dorotéia Joaquina de Seixas, Gonzaga's muse, died in Ouro Preto in 1853, when the first references to the rebellion were published.

Although it was alive in popular memory, the Inconfidência was a delicate subject for the cultured elite of the Second Reign. After all, the man who had proclaimed Brazilian independence was the grandson of Maria I, against whom the conspirators of the Inconfidência rebelled. The mad queen's great-grandson was governing the country. Brazil was a monarchy ruled by the house of Bragança, while the Inconfidência preached an American-style republic. It was not easy to exalt the so-called Inconfidentes, and Tiradentes in particular, without in some way condemning his executioners and the existing political system. It was not by chance that the first references to the rebellion came from a foreign historian, Robert Southey. His *History of Brazil* was published in 1810, and the Portuguese translation appeared in 1862. But the chapter on the Inconfidência, translated by Resende Costa, Jr., was published in the *Revista do Instituto Histórico e Geográfico* in 1846. The only source at Southey's disposal was the record of the court sentence. His analysis is neutral, referring to the Inconfidência as the first manifestation of revolutionary principles and practices in Brazil and criticizing the imperfection of the trial and the barbaric laws of the period. But he also records that the Portuguese government deserved praise for its clemency.[14]

The second reference to the Inconfidentes, which is far from neutral, is found in the book by Charles Ribeyrolles, *Brasil pitoresco* (Picturesque Brazil), published in Brazil in 1859. Unlike Southey, who was a friend to Portugal, Ribeyrolles was a radical republican from the days of the Paris uprising of 1848. He was deported from France in 1849 because of his political involvement. He arrived in Brazil in 1858 and made connections with republicans in Rio de Janeiro. In his analysis of the Inconfidência, also based on the record of the court sentence, Ribeyrolles does not conceal his sympathy for the rebels and his criticism of the Portuguese government. In his account, Tiradentes wears the true colors of a civic hero. He is the martyr capable of dying without any trace of fear, for "he sacrificed himself for a cause"—an interpretation typical of a French revolutionary. Although Ribeyrolles praises the climate of freedom in Pedro II's empire, which made possible the publication of his book, he attributes this freedom to the blood of Tiradentes, which, once shed, has germinated. A phrase about Tiradentes challenged Brazilian republicans and provoked the monarchy: "It would be weakness not to raise the cadaver that Portugal dragged through the dungeons."[15]

Brazilian literature took note of this theme before historiography did so. Gonzaga's *Liras* was published in the 1840s. The novel by Antônio Ferreira de Souza entitled *Gonzaga ou a conjuração de Tiradentes* (Gonzaga or the Conspiracy of Tiradentes) appeared in 1848. Bernardo Guimarães published his story "A cabeça de Tiradentes" (The Head of Tiradentes) in 1867. That same year, Castro Alves wrote the play *Gonzaga ou a Revolução de Minas* (Gonzaga or the Revolution of Minas), which was presented in 1866 in São Paulo, Salvador, and Rio de Janeiro. In this dramatic version, the character of Gonzaga is in the foreground, a choice that ignited a lengthy controversy about the leadership of the movement. But in the poem declaimed by the character Maria that concludes the play, Tiradentes appears in the idealized form that was gradually being imposed on him:

> Behold him, the giant of the square,
> The Christ of the masses!
> It is Tiradentes there . . .
> The Titan who passes![16]

The first political conflict revolving around Tiradentes apparently occurred in 1862, at the time of the inauguration of the statue of Pedro I in the then Largo do Rocio, or Constitution Square, today's Tiradentes Square. The occasion and the locale were the very embodiment of the conflict. In the place where Tiradentes was hanged, the government was erecting a statue to the grandson of the queen who ordered the infamous death. Teófilo Otoni, the liberal Minas leader of the 1842 revolt, called the statue a lie in bronze, and the expression became a republican battle cry. Inspired by Otoni, the liberal Pedro Luiz Pereira de Souza composed a poem to be distributed on the day of the statue's inauguration. The police confiscated the leaflets, but the poem survived and was republished in Ouro Preto in 1888. The text speaks of the popular expectations of the monument. Many hoped that it would be a dedication to Tiradentes. What was actually revealed, however, was the statue of Pedro I:

> In the days of cowardice
> Tyranny is celebrated
> And they make statues of kings.
> . . . .
> Today Brazil kneels
> And kneels in contrition
> Before the granite mass
> Of the First Emperor!

It speaks of the vile bronze, recalling the expression of Otoni's, and refers to Tiradentes:

> He was the first martyr
> Who died for the homeland.
> . . . .
> From Tiradentes's blood
> Sprang forth our salvation.

And it ends by saying that Tiradentes needs no statue, for we see him standing at the pillory surrounded by a halo of freedom and faith.[17]

The struggle between the memory of Pedro I, promoted by the government, and that of Tiradentes, the symbol of the republicans, gradually became emblematic of the battle between monarchy and republic. The conflict continued until the proclamation of the republic, when it then represented distinct republican groups. In 1893, the Tiradentes Club attempted to cover the statue of Pedro I for the celebrations of April 21. Protests followed, and the commemoration was canceled. In 1902, there was talk of erecting a monument on the spot where the hanging was believed to have taken place, more or less the present-day site of the Tiradentes School on Avenida Visconde do Rio Branco. The federal Chamber passed a law in 1892 ordering the expropriation of the site. The monument was finally constructed in front of the new Chamber building, which was inaugurated in 1926 under the name Tiradentes Palace. This location was the former site of the Old Jail, where the Inconfidente heard his death sentence and from which he was taken for execution. The statue of Pedro I remained where it was but now faced a civic coexistence with his rival: his square became known as Tiradentes Square.[18]

The struggle between the figures of Pedro I and Tiradentes exhibited a powerful symbolism. Its strongest expression can perhaps be found in an article by the republican abolitionist Luís Gama, in the inaugural issue of a journal commemorating the 21st of April that was published by the Tiradentes Club in 1882. The title of the article, "The Christ of the Multitudes Goes to the Gallows," is a direct reference to the final poem in the play by Castro Alves. Luís Gama took the parallel between Tiradentes and Christ even further. The gallows were equated to the cross; Rio de Janeiro to Jerusalem; Calvary to the Rocio, as seen in the illustration "21st of April." In addition to transforming the gallows into an altar, he transmuted the monument to Pedro I into an imperial gibbet. Instead of the gallows, or the new altar of the fatherland, a monument was constructed. Instead of the tragedy of the martyr, the comedy of the statue was exhibited.

The struggle in constructing the myth of Tiradentes reached one of its most important milestones in 1873, with the publication of Joaquim Norberto de Souza Silva's *História da Conjuração Mineira* (History of the Minas Gerais Conspiracy). The author, who headed a section of the Ministry of the Empire, had discovered in its archives the results of the inquiry, the *Autos da Devassa*. The *Memória do êxito que teve a conjuração de Minas* of an anonymous author, mentioned above, and Penaforte's statements also came into his hands. Souza Silva's work was a veritable revolution in the study of the Inconfidência. He worked on the documents for thirteen years. In 1860 he began reading parts of his work at the Historical and Geographical Institute, of which he was a member. The work was hastily published in 1873, as the author himself stated, because of the emergence of the republican movement in 1870. In 1872, two years after the *Republican Manifesto,* a monument to Tiradentes was proposed in Rio de Janeiro. Souza Silva declared his opposition to the idea. He considered Tiradentes a secondary figure and disagreed with the depiction of him as a martyr in white garb, a noose around his neck,

10. "21st of April,"
Revista Illustrada, April 19, 1890.

"as if the colonial government wished to make eternal its lesson of terror."[19] To justify his opposition, he rushed the book into print.

By revealing important documents that were previously unknown, Souza Silva's work became an obligatory reference for later studies of the Inconfidência, whether supporting or disclaiming the movement.[20] Although disguised as a historiographic dispute—with all authors claiming to seek "historical truth"—the debate was invariably characterized by the struggle around the myth of Tiradentes. It is this aspect of the question that interests me here. Souza Silva was immediately accused of being in the service of the monarchy, of attempting to discredit the Inconfidência, and of denigrating the historical figure of Tiradentes. He responded in 1881 in the pages of the *Revista do Instituto Histórico,* arguing that he based himself exclusively on the documents and that he wrote as a historian and not as a patriot—that is, as a detached observer and not as an impassioned partisan.[21]

His detachment was highly contentious, for Souza Silva was a civil servant, a dyed-in-the-wool monarchist, a friend of the major politicians of the empire (the book was dedicated to the viscount of Bom Retiro), and the vice president of the Historical and Geographical Institute, which was then a quasi-official institution closely linked to the emperor. The secretary of the institute, canon Fernandes Pinheiro, wrote that Souza Silva's intention for the work was "to render sincere homage to the exalted prince in whose kingdom truth shines in its entire splendor."[22] Although Souza Silva's revelations aroused great irritation, they were probably accurate from a historical point of view. They pertain to the transformations that, according to him, took place in the personality and behavior of Tiradentes as a result of the long imprisonment, repeated interrogations, and actions of the Franciscan friars. His patriotic ardor was allegedly replaced by religious fervor; the glorious gallows were transformed into an altar of sacrifice. According to Souza Silva, Tiradentes chose to die with a prayer on his lips instead of the shout of revolt—long live freedom!—that exploded from the mouths of the martyrs in Pernambuco in 1817 and 1824. The writer summarized the reasons for his disappointment in one sentence: "They arrested a patriot; they executed a friar."[23]

The republicans protested. They denied that Tiradentes had kissed the hands and feet of his executioner; they did not accept the version that he walked to the gallows soliloquizing with the crucifix; they did not believe that, in refusing to wear any clothes beneath the white tunic of the condemned, he had said that Our Lord also died naked for his sins.[24] In short, there was resistance to the idea that Tiradentes became a mystic during his time in prison, and that he lost the drive for patriotic rebellion that had made him the principal figure in the conspiracy. By disqualifying Tiradentes as a rebel, Souza Silva shifted the leadership of the Inconfidência to the judge (*ouvidor*) and poet Tomás Antônio Gonzaga. This meant that the hero was no longer a man of the people, but rather a representative of the elite; no longer a hanged man, but rather a simple exile. A monument to Gonzaga would not have the connotation (so shocking to Souza

Silva) of glorifying a man who was hanged, beheaded, and quartered; it would also be much more palatable to the reigning dynasty.

Souza Silva's position was well-grounded in the statements by Penaforte and the anonymous author of the *Memória*. According to his accusation, there were even attempts to adulterate the text of this memoir, which was deposited at the Historical and Geographical Institute. Someone inked out the expression "he kissed his feet," which referred to Tiradentes's reaction before the executioner, who was known as Capitania. It is perfectly possible that this Inconfidente really did transform into a mystic as a result of the traumatic experience in prison and of the Franciscan friars' veritable brainwashing. If that were so, his mention of the death of Christ, whom he wished to emulate; the kissing of his hangman's feet; the clear reference to Christ forgiving his executioners; and the march to the gallows while soliloquizing with the crucifix that the friars had placed between his bound hands would not be surprising.

However, both Souza Silva and his critics were mistaken in thinking that Tiradentes's mysticism destroyed his patriotic appeal or stripped him of his credentials as a civic hero. Following Souza Silva's revelations and perhaps the oral tradition itself, various plastic and literary representations and even political exaltations of Tiradentes utilized religious symbolism and comparisons to the figure of Christ with increasing frequency. If Ribeyrolles saw only the patriot, the soldier, and the civic hero who sacrificed himself for the love of an idea, Castro Alves now spoke of the Christ of the multitudes. Frequent religious references are found among the abundant materials gathered in the collections published annually on the 21st of April by the Tiradentes Club, starting in 1882, as in the article by Luís Gama mentioned above. An article in 1888, written by republicans in Minas Gerais, attributed to Tiradentes an even greater moral strength than that of Christ: While Christ had sweat blood, Tiradentes supposedly heard his sentence with greater serenity.[25]

The civic homage to Tiradentes intensified after the proclamation of the republic. The 21st of April was declared a national holiday in 1890, along with the 15th of November. Allusions to Christ also continued. Articles in *O Paiz* for April 21, 1891, speak of the "tenuous and diaphanous figure of the martyr of the Inconfidência—pale, surrounded by a halo serene, and gentle—like that of Jesus of Nazareth." The parade that became part of the commemorations of the 21st of April recalled the procession of the burial of Christ on Good Friday. Related analogies had already appeared in the first parade, held in 1890. The cortege began in the vicinity of the Old Jail, where Tiradentes was held prisoner, and continued to Tiradentes Square; from there, it came to the Itamaraty Palace, where Deodoro greeted the celebrants. Representatives of the abolitionist and republican clubs, students, soldiers, and members of the Center for the Workers' Party accompanied the procession. The positivists took prominent positions, carrying a bust of the martyr sculpted by Almeida Reis on a litter. The mysterious Club of the Sons of Thalma was also present. It was a celebration of the passion (the Old Jail), death (Tiradentes Square), and resurrection (Itamaraty) of the new Christ. In later celebrations, the procession included a cart, which served to recall the one that transported the body of the "holy victim" after the hanging in 1792. It was the "burial" of the new Via Sacra.

During the parade of 1890, the positivist painter Décio Villares distributed a lithograph presenting the bust of Tiradentes with a rope around his neck and embellished with the palm of martyrs and the laurel leaves of victory. With his long hair and a beard and gazing into infinity, he was the very image of Christ. According to *O Paiz*, the lithograph represented the great martyr "just as his [Villares's] poetic fantasy and his patriotic spirit designed him."[26] Without a doubt, Villares's idealization went considerably beyond the positivist aesthetic, with its tendency to idealize heroes.

If there was ever a portrait of Tiradentes done by those who personally knew him, it did not survive. The dominant view when Décio Villares created his lithograph was the traditional, tendentious description of Tiradentes taken from the book by Souza Silva. Based on the statement by Alvarenga Peixoto and taken from the *Autos da Devassa*, Souza Silva described Tiradentes as "ugly and frightened," and contributed his own belief that there was nothing appealing about him; that he was repellent. Those disputing this description appeared much later.

11. Décio Villares, *Tiradentes,*
lithograph, Positivist Church of Brazil.

Villares's interpretation, which openly contradicted the supposed true version, thus became more important. In 1928, Villares depicted Tiradentes once again, this time in an oil painting. (See fig. III.) In this work, clearly more developed than the first, the powerful colors and the heightened stylization of the figure—the hair and beard are less unruly—accentuated the resemblance to Christ, or at least the sweet Christ portrayed in most representations, even more strongly than in the lithograph.[27]

Christian symbolism appeared in several other art works of the period. In the painting *Martyrdom of Tiradentes,* by Aurélio de Figueiredo (see fig. II), the observer's perspective is that of looking up at the martyr, who poses on the gallows as one crucified; with a friar at his feet handing him a crucifix, and the hangman, Capitania, kneeling and covering his face with his hand. It is a foot-of-the-cross scene. Even in the somewhat shocking representation by Pedro Américo, the allusion to Christ is inescapable. (See fig. IV.) His *Tiradentes Quartered,* from 1893, depicts the body parts lying on the gibbet as if it were an altar. The head, with a long red beard, is placed in the highest position with a crucifix beside it, clearly suggesting the resemblance between the two dramas. One arm dangles outside the scaffold as an explicit allusion to Michelangelo's *Pietà.*

Aside from the obvious appeal to the Christian tradition of the Brazilian people, which helped to further transmit the image of the civic Christ, one could inquire about other reasons behind Tiradentes's success as a republican hero. It was not without resistance that he attained such a position. The figure of Tiradentes faced other historical competitors for the title of hero of the new regime, as well as rivals from the events of November 15. The most notable historical competitors included the leaders of the Ragamuffins' War in the south of Brazil, and the respected figure of Frei Caneca in the north. That there is no evidence of any effort to transform Bento Gonçalves, president of the Rio Grande do Sul republic, into a republican national hero is perhaps due to the peculiar position of Rio Grande do Sul in the Brazilian scene and the suspicion of separatism directed at the Ragamuffins' revolt. The *gaúcho* heroes lacked the national character indispensable to the image of a republican hero.

Frei Caneca was a more serious contender. The hero of two up-risings, one for independence and the other against the absolutism of the first emperor, he also died a martyr's death: he was shot, for no hangman offered his services to execute him. Souza Silva censured Tiradentes precisely for not having died like the martyrs of 1817 and 1824, who carried defiance on their lips and the cry of freedom in their throats—authentic, civic heroes. In various talks at the Tira-dentes Club, the fact was mentioned that the hero from Minas Gerais was not the only republican martyr, nor the first. Frei Caneca was sometimes cited as commanding such respect.

Without a doubt, geography was one of the factors that may have led to Tiradentes's victory. Tiradentes was the hero of the region that, from the mid-nineteenth century to the present, was considered the political center of the country: Minas Gerais, Rio de Janeiro, and São Paulo, or the three *capitanias* that he initially sought to make in-dependent. Republicanism was also strongest and the Tiradentes clubs most numerous in this region. At the end of the nineteenth century, Brazil's northern region, in contrast, was in an economic and political decline, and it was not known for the vigor of its republican movement. In addition, the Confederation of the Equator of 1824 also showed separatist tendencies that blemished it as a national movement. If it is true that the Inconfidência sought the liberation of only three *capitanias,* it was based not on any separatist idea but rather on a tactical calculation. Once those three were free, the rest would likely follow.

It appears to me, however, that the preference for Tiradentes is based on still another important element. It is possible that his ad-vantage lay precisely in Souza Silva's criticism. Frei Caneca and his comrades were engaged in two very real struggles, in which there was bloodshed and death. Frei Caneca died, almost arrogantly, as a confrontational hero in a cold military ritual of shooting. He was a rebellious, accusatory, and aggressive martyr. He died neither as a victim nor as a bearer of the pains of a people. He died as a civic leader, not as a religious martyr, although, ironically, he was a friar.

Tiradentes was exactly the opposite: the patriot turned mystic. The courage that he demonstrated—Friar Penaforte said he was "strong of heart"—came, in the end, from religious rather than civic fervor. He explicitly assumed the role of martyr, identifying himself openly with Christ. The ceremonial of the hanging, the scaffold, the gallows raised to an unusual height, the presence of soldiers, the observing multitude—everything contributed to parallel the two events and the two figures: the Crucifixion and the hanging, Christ and Tiradentes. The subsequent quartering, the shed blood, and the distribution of body parts along the paths he traversed also furthered the symbolism of sowing the martyr's blood, which, as Tertullian said, was the seed of the Christian church.

This may be one of the principal secrets of Tiradentes's success. The fact that the conspiracy never moved into the phase of concrete action spared him from shedding another's blood, from committing violence against others, and from creating enemies. Tiradentes was "the ideal martyr, immaculate in the whiteness of the robe of the condemned."[28] The true violence was that of the executioners. He was the victim of a dream, an ideal, and of "the mad desires of a dreamed-of freedom," as expressed by the author of the *Memória*. He was the victim not only of the Portuguese government and its representatives but also of his friends. Joaquim Silvério, a personal friend who betrayed Tiradentes, became the new Judas. Tiradentes was also a victim of the co-conspirators who, like new Peters, displayed their cowardice by trying to place on him all the blame—blame that he willingly assumed. He congratulated his friends when their death sentence was commuted; he was content to go alone to the gallows. (See fig. V.) Explicitly, like the Christ whom he would emulate in his nakedness and in the pardoning of his hangman, he took on himself the blame, the pain, and the dreams of his companions and his compatriots. Through his self-sacrifice, he achieved in the mystical domain the salvation that was beyond his reach in the civic domain.

All of this penetrated deeply into a popular feeling marked by Christian religiosity. Everyone could identify with the figure of Tiradentes; it engendered the mystical unity of the citizenry, the sense of participation, of union around an ideal, whether it was freedom, independence, or the republic. He was the civic totem. He antagonized no one; he did not divide people and social classes; he did not divide the country, nor did he separate the present from the past or the future. On the contrary, he linked the republic to independence and projected it as the ideal of greater freedom in the future— freedom, however late in coming, as it was written in the flag of the Inconfidentes.

The strongest aversion to making a myth out of Tiradentes, as we observed before, came from the monarchists who defended Pedro I. This aversion merits further attention, for it indicates certain nuances not yet mentioned in this analysis. Or rather, it indicates certain phases in the construction of the myth and the persistence of ambiguity in its content. First, Tiradentes was presented as a republican hero, which surely antagonized the monarchists and divided the citizenry. Further, he was the hero of the republican propagandists and clubs, and he was popular in nature. He was not only a republican hero but also a hero for the Jacobins, the party's most radical sector. At the time of the proclamation of the republic, the Tiradentes Club of Rio de Janeiro, the main organizer of his homage, was led by Sampaio Ferraz, who was linked to the radical propagandists. Tiradentes's republicanism was highlighted, but so was his humble, plebeian, and popular character, which contrasted with those of his companions, who were part of the economic and cultural elite of Minas Gerais. Tiradentes became synonymous with republican radicalism and, to some degree, Florianism. As such, his figure represented a strong opposition to the monarchical symbol, represented by the statue of Pedro I.

The conflict of 1893 was a watershed. It signified both a sudden shift in the republic's direction and a change in the image of the hero. It was made even more significant by taking place in the Floriano period, during which another Jacobin, the physician Barata Ribeiro, occupied the mayoralty of the capital. The incident brought the two Jacobins, previously allies, into opposition: Sampaio Ferraz in the Tiradentes Club and Barata Ribeiro as mayor. The mayor had authorized the plans to cover the statue of Pedro I, but he retreated when faced with the strong resistance generated by the idea. The resistance came not only from what could be called the greatest conservative press of the era, the *Jornal do Commercio*, but also from the unofficial republican organ, Bocaiúva's *O Paiz*. The editor of *O Paiz* attributed the club's idea to demagoguery, intolerance, and radicalism. The best republicans, he said, were those who at the moment contributed to reconciliation and not to division. Barata Ribeiro eventually accepted these views and ordered the demolition of the bandstand that enclosed the statue. In protest, the club canceled the commemorations, and Sampaio Ferraz resigned as its leader.

A Tiradentes battalion, both Florianist and Jacobin in nature, was formed during the Naval Revolt at the end of 1893. The battalion was dissolved in 1897, amid the governmental reaction to the Jacobin agitation that culminated in an assassination attempt against the president of the republic. It was allowed to reorganize in 1902, during the administration of Campos Sales, after fervent sentiments had diminished. That year marked the official initialization of plans for constructing the Tiradentes monument, which, as we already know, was erected in a different location to avoid the confrontation with Pedro I.[29]

The 1893 episode indicated the conditions for the acceptance of the republican hero as a national hero: elimination of the radical Jacobin image, the Frei Caneca version, and even the Florianist version. To consolidate itself as a government, the republic needed to eliminate its rough edges, reconcile itself with the monarchical past, and incorporate different currents of republicanism. Tiradentes was seen not as a radical republican hero but as a civic-religious hero, as a martyr, a uniter, and a bearer of the image of an entire people.

This was already the insight of the artists who represented him as Christ. The ideal of universal representation of the nation preceded that of the republic. A poem written by a worker in 1884 contained the following lines:

> The duty of Brazilians,
> Whatever their view,
> Is this day to unite
> And pay homage to you.
> So, you royalists
> And you anarchists,

Join the positivists,
Hearts beating as one.[30]

The same poem—written, we should recall, before the abolition of slavery—ends by linking Tiradentes to the struggle against slavery: "Broken, the slaves' / fetters will be as poems / to that immortal genius." The interpretation of the Inconfidência as an abolitionist movement, not merely a liberating and republican one, linked Tiradentes to the three principal transformations undergone by the country: independence from Portugal, the abolition of slavery, and the establishment of a republic. Of the positivists' civic trinity, Tiradentes alone could subsume and represent all three movements. He was accepted by the monarchists, provided Pedro I was not excluded; by abolitionists, whether republicans or monarchists; and by republicans.

The worker's poem further suggested the acceptance of Tiradentes by anarchists, a thesis that perhaps the anarchist movement at the turn of the century would not have endorsed. But the non-anarchist organized labor movement and even the socialists easily accepted the homage of Tiradentes. It is worth remembering that, in the first public celebration of the 21st of April following the proclamation of the republic, representatives of the Directorate of the Workers Party were among the participants in the procession. Vicente de Souza, who was a socialist with positivist leanings, an activist in organizing workers' parties and in publishing workers' newspapers such as the *Echo Popular*, and later one of the principals in the revolt against compulsory vaccination, when he led the Working Class Center, appeared as one of the orators at the festivities promoted by the Tiradentes Club.

At the end of the empire, or the beginning of the republic, even monarchists began claiming for themselves the heritage of Tiradentes. Writing after the proclamation of the republic, the viscount Taunay complained of the monopoly that the republicans, especially the Jacobins, were trying to maintain on the memory of this hero. By gaining the country's independence, he asserted, the empire had realized Tiradentes's dream. For that reason, "he also belongs to us."[31]

The acceptance of Tiradentes thus was accompanied by his transformation into a national hero rather than a republican hero. He united the country across time, geography, and class. For this, his image had to be idealized, as it actually was. This process was aided by the lack of a genuine portrait or description of him, not withstanding a few indications in the documents of the trial. His semblance was idealized not only by positivist artists such as Décio Villares and Eduardo de Sá, but also by cartoonists in the illustrated magazines of the period. To positivists, the idealization of heroes was a rule of Comtean aesthetics; to others, it was merely part of the attempt to generate the myth and cult of the hero.

This effort was acutely perceived by Ubaldino do Amaral Fontoura, the official orator of the 1894 celebrations held by the Tiradentes Club. He conceded the existence of rivals for the position of precursor of Brazilian nationality and the republic. But the republic, he said, challenges whoever would topple the legend that had been a century in the making. Nor was he concerned with Tiradentes's physical characteristics. "It was perhaps a fortunate thing that this Christ left behind no shroud. Each artist has given him a different face." He was represented, Ubaldino added, with the gentleness of Jesus, with traits of ancient heroes, and even as a *caboclo*, or backwoodsman. In the statue erected by the republican government of Minas Gerais in Ouro Preto, he has the carriage of a prophet or demigod. Ubaldino concluded by commenting on the artists: "None of them was correct, and all were correct, because it is from this that legends are made."[32]

The attempt to transform Tiradentes into a national hero adapted to all tastes did not entirely eliminate the ambiguity of the symbol. The republican government tried to appropriate it by declaring April 21 a national holiday and by constructing a statue in front of the building that housed the Chamber of Deputies in 1926. The recent military governments took further steps. A 1965 law declared Tiradentes the civic patron of the Brazilian nation and ordered his portrait placed in all government offices. During Getúlio Vargas's dictatorial Estado Novo, officially supported plays exalted Tiradentes.[33] During this period (1940), the traditional representation, or the

12. Francisco Andrade, *Tiradentes,*
statue, Rio de Janeiro.

Nazarene style, was modified. José Walsht Rodrigues, a specialist in military uniforms and a collaborator with the Integralist Gustavo Barroso, painted Tiradentes as an *alferes,* or second lieutenant, in the Sixth Company of the Dragoons Regiment. (See fig. VI.) The civic hero thus became a professional military man.[34]

From the Jacobins to the guerrilla movements of the 1970s, one of which adopted his name, the left also embraced Tiradentes. In the 1940s, Portinari retained the religious symbolism in his painting of Tiradentes. His *Os despojos de Tiradentes no caminho novo das Minas* (The Remains of Tiradentes on the New Road to Minas) shows pieces of Tiradentes's body hanging from posts and kneeling women, recalling the scene at Calvary. In the 1960s, the Arena Theater also revived Tiradentes's subversive image.[35]

The secret of the vitality of this hero lies, perhaps, in this very ambiguity and in its resistance to incessant efforts to "quarter" his memory.

chapter four

THE REPUBLIC AS A WOMAN

Mary or Marianne?

Representing the republic by the allegorical figure of a woman was one of the telling elements of French republican imagery. The monarchy was fittingly represented by the figure of the king, who stood for the nation itself. Once the monarchy was overthrown and the king beheaded, new symbols were needed to simultaneously fill the figurehead void and to represent new ideas and ideals, such as revolution, liberty, the republic, and the *patria* itself. Among the many adapted symbols and allegories, most of which were inspired by the classical tradition, the feminine figure stands out. From the First Republic to the Third, the allegorical female, whether representing liberty, revolution, or the republic, dominates French civic symbolism.

The feminine figure began to be employed as soon as the republic was declared in 1792. The inspiration came from Rome, where a woman was the symbol of freedom. The first seal of the republic bore the effigy of a woman standing, dressed in Roman garb, and holding in her right hand a spear from whose point hung the cap of liberty. Her left hand held a bundle of arms, and a rudder complemented the symbolism. The cap of liberty identified the freedmen of ancient Rome; the bundle of arms indicated unity or fraternity; the rudder, the government. The spear, the people's weapon par excellence, stood for the populace in the fledging regime. The female figure also appeared in living allegories; for instance, a young woman represented liberty in the Festival of the Supreme Being in 1794. In the Place de la Révolution, a statue of liberty in the form of a woman, standing with a cap of liberty on her head and a spear in her right hand, presided over the executions by guillotine. Undoubtedly, Manon Roland was addressing her when, shortly before being executed, he exclaimed: "O Liberty, how many crimes are committed in thy name!"[1]

The events of 1830 stood out in history for several reasons. One was the painting by Eugène Delacroix, entitled *Liberty Leading the People* (fig. VII). A masterpiece of world art, the canvas depicts liberty represented by a female figure with the features of the people. The cap of liberty covers her hair, which is pulled back. In her right hand is another republican symbol, the tricolor flag, which was abandoned during the Restoration and later adopted by Louis Philippe, after receiving it from Lafayette, the same person who had officially sanctioned it in 1790. In her left hand is a rifle with fixed bayonet. Her naked, aggressive breasts stand out, as does her forceful gesture of command amid the dead and wounded of the Paris barricades. She could be singing the *Marseillaise*. The strength of the painting lies in its combination of elements of idealization, such as the naked breasts and feet, with characteristics of great verisimilitude. Delacroix, as is well known, was inspired by an actual combatant, Marie Deschamps, who had acquitted herself in a noteworthy fashion in the fighting at one of the barricades in July 1830. The fact that the painting was, at the same time, one of the principal works—if not *the* principal work—of romanticism also contributed to its impact.

Shortly after Delacroix painted this work, François Rudé carved into one of the pillars of the Arch of Triumph at the Place de l'Étoile a highly expressive scene in which the idealized and belligerent figure of a woman is leading fighters into battle. The tableau, originally called *The Departure of the Volunteers,* came to be known as *The Marseillaise* due to the powerful portrayal of its central figure. Rudé's bas-relief, although more stylized, has the same meaning as Delacroix's painting: the figure of a woman—reality or symbol, reality and

13. François Rudé, *The Departure of the Volunteers,*
Place de l'Étoile, Paris.

symbol—represents the struggles and the ideals of the revolution, the republic, and the *patria*.

The proclamation of the Second Republic in 1848 reawakened interest in republican symbols. In a competition that was held to select a symbol for the Second Republic, a large majority of painters and sculptors chose to use the female figure.[2] Despite the disappointing artistic quality of the competition, a few works have survived, among them that of Honoré Daumier, in which the republic is represented by a woman nursing two children. She is no longer the warlike figure of Delacroix and Rudé: Daumier paints a republic-woman who is maternal, protective, sure, and strong. She is seated, holding the tricolor in her right hand, while her left hand supports one of the children that nurses on her vast, generous breasts. According to Maurice Agulhon, a schism is already evident in the feminine representation of the republic, which would thenceforth continue to grow. One can already distinguish a bourgeois republic from a socialist republic. Although the feminine figure is retained, the distinction manifests itself both by the manner in which the woman is represented (seated or standing, maternal or combative, hair combed or unruly, breasts covered or bare) and by her accompanying attributes. Among these, the most telling is the presence or absence of the cap of liberty. Always red in color, the cap becomes one of the principal indicators of radicalism, while the tricolor flag gradually turns into a sign of moderation, or a sign of a respectable republic. Note in Daumier's portrait the seated posture, the presence of the tricolor, and the absence of the cap. The Second Republic also introduced the feminine figure as a symbol on coins, in heraldry, and on postage stamps. In all of these, however, the cap of liberty is absent. On coats of arms, it is replaced by a halo in the form of solar rays, an image later immortalized by Frederic Auguste Bartholdi in the Statue of Liberty presented to New York City.

It was in the period preceding the Third Republic, however, that the figure of a woman became popularized in representations of the republic, in opposition to the empire of Napoleon III. The popularization involved the figure of Marianne, a popular name for French women. Marianne came to personify the republic and unify

14. Honoré Daumier,
The Republic.

the earlier forms of representation. Statuettes, busts, and engravings of Marianne spread throughout the country, especially in southern France. In response, the government encouraged the worship of the Virgin Mary. There was a battle between the forms of worship, which Agulhon felicitously phrased as Mariolatry versus Mariannolatry. Marianne worship found its most exaggerated form in Félix Pyat's *Letter to Marianne,* published in London in 1856. At one point, Pyat exclaimed: "For us, the proscribed republicans, ... thou art all: refuge, city, home, our family, our mother, our love, our faith, our hope, the idol to which we sacrifice even our memory, the ideal for which we live and die happily." The letter ends with a Hail Mary or, rather, a Hail Marianne: "Hail, Marianne, full of strength, the people are with thee, blessed is the fruit of thy womb, the Republic etc."[3]

With the Paris Commune and the Third Republic, what was a clandestine and persecuted cult became open and official. Once the

Third Republic was consolidated, great monuments depicting the feminine figure appeared. But the schism that had first emerged in 1848 now took on an ever clearer definition as relations between the republic and socialism became more complicated. New revolutionary symbols appeared, such as the worker naked to the waist.[4] Marianne herself underwent a change in meaning. From a symbol of the liberating republic, she became a symbol of the nation, or France itself. She had moved to the political right. In the end, the feminine figure ceased to be used as a symbol of the French republic. The republic itself had no more monuments.

The French-oriented Brazilian republicans therefore had a great wealth of images and symbols in which to find inspiration. What interests me here is their use of the allegorical female figure. They had a slight disadvantage when compared to the French. While the monarchy in France was masculine, the heiress to the throne and regent-presumptive in Brazil was a woman, Princess Isabel. This disadvantage, however, was lessened by efforts to nullify Isabel's standing by showing that she was a mere puppet in the hands of Count d'Eu. At the same time, a systematic campaign was mounted to discredit the count. In São Paulo, a humorous republican newspaper was founded for that purpose. Silva Jardim followed the count on a trip to the north of the country, where he sought to neutralize the count's campaign in favor of a third imperial reign.[5] The fact that the count was French only made easier the task of identifying him with the *ancien régime*. Silva Jardim did not hesitate to propose for him the same fate that the French Revolution reserved for Louis XVI. Thus, a way was made for a republican appropriation of the feminine image.[6]

The initial effort was by cartoonists in the press, the great majority of whom were sympathetic to the republic. Feminine representations appeared even before the proclamation, as demonstrated in the political cartoon by Angelo Agostini in the *Revista Illustrada* for June 9, 1888. The same allegory can be seen in the cartoon of November 16, 1889, drawn by Pereira Neto (see fig. 28, next chapter).[7] Pereira Neto continued for several years to reproduce this feminine image, wearing Roman garb, with her feet bare or wearing sandals, with the cap of liberty, and usually carrying the new flag in one hand.

15. Angelo Agostini, "Slave Owners Ask the Republic for Indemnification,"
Revista Illustrada, June 9, 1888.

See also, for example, his cartoon in the issue dated December 14,
1889. Here, the Brazilian republic fraternizes with her Argentine
sister. The two republics are represented by women who are similar
in every way except for the flags.

At times, the feminine figure took on bellicose aspects. One curious example is that of the figure that appeared in *O Mequetrefe* for
November 17, 1889. It takes little effort to see in it a copy of Rudé's
The Marseillaise. But generally, the bellicosity was merely indicated
by a sword, as in the drawing in no. 729 of the *Revista Illustrada* in
1897, in which the republic-woman salutes the dead of the Canudos
campaign. Everything obeyed the classical model: Athena assumed
her original warrior countenance and thus abandoned, for a time, her
role as protector of the peace. The most complete instance of a warrior image of the republic appeared in *O Malho* for November 26,
1904 (fig. VIII). There, the republic, dressed in the battle armor of
Athena, crushes the revolt that had just broken out in Rio de Janeiro.

16. Pereira Neto, "December 8, 1889,"
Revista Illustrada, December 14, 1889.

17. "Proclamation of the Federative Brazilian Republic,"
O Mequetrefe, November 17, 1889.

The same type of representation was long used in *O Paiz,* the semi-official newspaper run by Quintino Bocaiúva. Here, Julião Oliveira upheld the stylized figure from antiquity even though, with the start of a new century, most of his colleagues were beginning to ridicule the new regime by their characterization of the feminine figure. Until the end of the nineteenth century, however, newspapers and magazines did not diverge from the model established by the *Revista Illustrada.*

With the exception of Décio Villares (see fig. IX), painters all but ignored feminine symbolism in their representations of the new regime. Perhaps the only canvas worthy of mention is that by the Bahian Manuel Lopes Rodrigues entitled *Allegory of the Republic.* The work is from 1896 and was executed in Rome, where the painter had been living since before the proclamation of the republic. The artist undoubtedly used a live model, but in all other ways, the image approximates the stylization of the cartoonists. The clothing—tunic and cape—is classical, as are the sandals. Some of the symbols are classical as well: palms, laurel leaves (or coffee branches, as in this case), a sword, and the Medusa's head medallion (used by Athena on her shield or her breastplate). It is a typical representation of the Second Republic of 1848, when the French government requested that she be depicted seated, giving an impression of tranquility, peace, and security. In order to represent the Brazilian republic in this fashion in 1896, it was necessary for the painter to reside outside the country.[8] With the exception of this painting by a little-known artist, no other works of value exist. The Brazilian republic inspired no David, no Delacroix, and no Daumier. Nor did its sculpture produce a Rudé. There are busts of women representing the republic, some of them housed in the Museum of the Republic in Rio de Janeiro. They are more creative, less stylized works in which the female figure always appears in the cap of liberty and varies from the civic and sometimes bellicose to the sensual. Their effect on the popular imagination was probably minimal, for they are refined works for domestic display, office pieces. They may recall the busts of Marianne, but with the difference that the latter, before 1870, were barred from public exhibition by censorship. Still, whenever possible, these busts were borne

18. Manuel Lopes Rodrigues,
Allegory of the Republic.

in processions through the streets and displayed in the windows of houses.

The positivist artists merit separate mention. Their use of the feminine figure was based on a system of interpreting the world in which the republic was only one part, albeit an important part. In the positivist scale of values, humanity came first, followed by the *patria* and the family. The republic was the ideal organizational form for the country; woman ideally represented humanity. Comte believed that only altruism (a word he coined) could serve as basis for living together in the new positivist society without God. "Woman" best represented this sentiment and should thus be the ideal symbol of humanity. The perfect symbol would be the virgin mother, suggesting a mankind capable of reproduction without outside interference. Comte went so far as to specify the feminine type that should represent humanity: a thirty-year-old woman holding a child in her arms. He even expressed the wish that the face of his adored Clotilde de Vaux be used as the model and that it appear on all Western flags.[9]

Brazilian positivist artists, especially Décio Villares and Eduardo de Sá, were the only ones in the world of the plastic arts who were politically militant. Among their various works were paintings, sculptures, and monuments. The female figure is omnipresent, although, as mentioned above, it represents humanity and sometimes the *patria* more than it represents the republic. But even in France there were frequent shifts in the meaning of the feminine figure. The republic, the revolution, freedom, and the *patria* were often interchanged. Thus it is not unreasonable to include humanity in this list.[10]

In 1890, Décio Villares put Comte's wish into practice by painting the figure of humanity with the face of Clotilde de Vaux in his *Banner of Humanity,* which appeared in the cortege dedicated to the memory of Tiradentes. A protective figure, with her child at her bosom, the woman is, as Comte wished, every bit a mother (see fig. X).[11] The same characterization appears in the positivist-inspired monuments in Rio de Janeiro and Porto Alegre discussed in chapter 2. In Décio Villares's depiction of Benjamin Constant, the feminine figure conforms to Comte's specifications and dominates the construction. The figure of the hero is still under the protection of

19. Umberto Cavina,
Bust of the Republic,
Museum of the Republic.

20. *The Republic,*
unidentified artist,
Museum of the Republic.

another feminine figure, representing the country, which wraps him in the republican flag. Medallions in bas-relief by Eduardo de Sá show Constant's wife, Maria Joaquina; Comte's Clotilde; and Dante's Beatrice. Constant is a blessed man among women.

The monument to Floriano, the work of Eduardo de Sá, also exhibits two prominent female figures, although with more flexible symbolism. Eduardo de Sá opted for a less orthodox use of feminine figures, both in the symbolism they intended to convey and in their physical forms. One of the two young women, found at Floriano's side, is the future of the country; the other, dominating one entire side of the monument, is love, or the integration of races in Brazil. Although they are clothed, as Comte wished, both show the exuberance of their physical form, especially the breasts. In the monument to Júlio de Castilhos, Décio Villares once again placed the feminine figure at the top as a direct image of the republic.

21. Monument to Benjamin
Constant, detail.

Positivist painters did not cling to classical models, even if their
aesthetic ideas were close to those of Jacques-Louis David. In this
respect, they had an advantage over the cartoonists. But if they es-
caped from Pallas Athena, it was to fall into the trap of Clotilde de
Vaux. Their allegorical feminine figures also departed from Brazilian
models. This fact is even more disappointing when we recall the importance given by the positivists to the black race, which they considered superior to whites, and to the incorporation of the Indians and
the proletariat into the Brazilian nation. Décio Villares, in an indis-
putable exception, was the only painter of the time to exalt the black
race, as in his *African Epopée in Brazil*. But when it came to representing humanity or the republic, Indians, blacks, mulattos, or proletarians were neither depicted nor idealized. Instead the choice was
Clotilde, with or without the cap of liberty.

22. Monument to
Floriano Peixoto, detail.

The positivist painters were the only ones who seriously attempted to use the feminine figure as civic allegory, with the proviso that the allegory preferably referred to humanity. It can be said that the attempt to imitate the French effort to sell the new regime by means of the feminine image was meager and ended in a resounding failure. Nor did the transformation of the Imperial Academy of Fine Arts into the National School of Fine Arts, then under the direction of H. Bernardelli, with the subsequent exclusion of artists identified with the *ancien régime,* appear to have effected any major change. The republic produced no aesthetic of its own, nor did it seek to politically redefine the use of the existing aesthetic, as did David. The positivists were an isolated instance. Historically based paintings were still done, when done at all, in the same molds as those of Pedro Américo and Vítor Meireles. It is symptomatic, for example, that in the art salons that were promoted after the advent of the republic and after the creation of the National School of Fine Arts, almost nothing appeared that reflected either the use of the feminine allegory or the civic exaltation of the new regime by other means. In general, historical painting lost ground after the proclamation of the new regime. The few civic canvases that were produced limited themselves to attempts at creating republican heroes, as in the case of Deodoro and Tiradentes, or to celebrating the new institutions, such as the constitution of 1891.[12]

In fact, cartoonists quickly began using the feminine figure to ridicule the republic. Enemies of the republic in France did the same. The virgin or the heroic woman of the republicans was easily transformed into a woman of the streets, a prostitute. The difference was that in Brazil, compared to France, this was the dominant representation, used even by those who initially supported the new regime. Disappointment, as reflected in the well-known phrase "This is not the republic of my dreams," rapidly found its way into the world of the cartoonists, at the same time that it reached the politicians and writers of propaganda.

In the first decade of the new republic, the criticisms were timid in nature. In the magazine *D. Quixote* of November 25, 1895, Angelo Agostini depicts the republic as a downcast woman mounted on a small donkey, facing backwards, while the other republics of the Americas gallop toward progress (see fig. 30, next chapter). With the turn of the century, especially in *O Malho,* the criticism became general and merciless. C. do Amaral, in *O Malho* of November 15, 1902, shows the contrast between the republic dreamed of in 1889 and that of 1902. The former is represented by an innocent young woman; the latter by a mature woman with a debauched gaze, exhaling cigarette smoke. In the following year, Raul, also in *O Malho,* represents the republic as a bedridden woman whose husband, at her side, comments that it has been thirteen years and she still has not gotten up. J. Carlos, in *O Filhote* of November 11, 1909 (dates close to the 15th of November were preferred for criticism), exhibits an openly prostituted republic involved in an orgy with politicians of the time, while the ghost of Benjamin Constant displays amazement that at the age of twenty she is already so debauched. K. Lixto, in *Fon-Fon!* of

23. C. do Amaral, "Mlle. Republic, Who Today Completes
Another *Spring*," *O Malho*, November 15, 1902.

24. Raul, "The 15th of November,"
O Malho, November 14, 1903.

November 13, 1913, also depicts the republic as prematurely aged and decadent, to the surprise of the old monarchy. Finally, to avoid excessive examples (which would be easy to supply), Vasco Lima, in *O Gato* of March 22, 1913, presents a republic that is the Brazilian version of Daumier's painting. Daumier's republic-mother— protective and nourishing—retains in Vasco Lima's caricature the exaggeratedly huge breasts; and when faced with the incredulous reaction of Marshal Hermes, the artist justifies the detail by saying, "It's the raw nudity of truth. The Republic nurses so many people!" Instead of a mother, the republic is the wet nurse or the milk cow that must feed politicians and functionaries who live off of her rather than for her.

The most scandalous example of the discrediting of the republic by means of female representation came from a minister of the Campos Sales administration. In 1900, Fausto Cardoso, a member of the Chamber of Deputies, denounced the treasury minister, Joaquim Murtinho, on the chamber floor as "a man who orders depicted on treasury notes and currency, as the symbol of the Republic, the portrait of prostitutes." According to the accusation, which, although it provoked a tumult in the chamber and led to the suspension of the session, went uncontested, the photo was that of a Mrs. Prates, one of the best-known prostitutes in the capital. According to other versions, it was that of Laurinda Santos Lobo, Murtinho's niece and lover. On the reverse of the note, the republic was represented by a classical figure, Pallas Athena with helmet, shield, and spear. The note constitutes a priceless encapsulation: the republic, when not represented by classical or romantic abstraction, found its face only in the version of the fallen woman; it was a *res publica*, in the sense that a prostitute was a public woman.[13]

References to the new regime found in literature frequently take the same direction. The bohemian Neiva, in Coelho Neto's novel *Fogo fátuo,* is unresigned to the proclamation of the republic and to the measures of the provisional government. To him, everything appears false and ridiculous. He especially dislikes the presidential regime. The country, he says, is a virtuous woman who doesn't change husbands. She remarries only upon becoming a widow. She can't live in concubinage, with one man today, another tomorrow.[14]

25. K. Lixto, "The 15th of November," *Fon-Fon!*, November 13, 1913.

26. Vasco Lima, "This Is Not a Republic," *O Gato*, March 22, 1913.

27. Treasury note of two *mil-réis*, 1900.

The view of the republic as a prostitute is evident in *História do Brasil pelo método confuso* (History of Brazil by the Confused Method) by Mendes Fradique. In this simultaneously hilarious and lucid version of history, the Republic, a poor damsel oppressed by tyranny, is saved by Don Quixote, who invades the general headquarters in search of her. To the nobleman's surprise, he confronts an orgiastic scene in which the prominent figure is "a semi-nude woman, with a cigarette in the corner of her mouth, the type characteristic of a Montmartre *divette*." Scandalized, he learns from the historian Oliveira Lima that said lady is the Republic. Despite the disappointment, Don Quixote introduces her to the Brazilian people, declaring his mission accomplished. He laments only that he was unable to hand her over as he intended: "Safe and virgin."[15]

How does one explain the failure of the positive representation of the republic as a woman? The search for an explanation can take several directions, but the core of the question may lie in Baczko's already cited observation that in order to create roots, the imagery, despite being manipulable, needs a community of imagination or a community of meaning. Symbols, allegories, and myths take root in a hospitable and fertile social and cultural terrain. Lacking such suitable grounds, any attempt to create, to manipulate, and to use them as elements of legitimization falls into the void, if not into ridicule. It is my impression that in France there was such a community of imagination, whereas in Brazil, there was not.

In France, women had genuine roles in the Revolution, or, rather, the revolutions—including those of 1789, 1830, 1848, and 1871. There were numerous women in the crowd that stormed the Bastille in 1789. About four thousand of them marched to Versailles a few months later to take the king back to Paris. Some, such as Saint-Milhier's nameless heroine and citizens Bourgougnoux and Marie Charpentier, distinguished themselves by heroic acts and became the first living symbols of the republic. Other figures shortly followed suit: Olympe de Gouges, who was guillotined in 1793, Pauline Léon, and Claire Lacombe. The latter organized the Revolutionary Republican Women's Club. In actuality, this club was so revolutionary that it was not accepted by the male-dominated Convention. Théroigne de Mericourt organized battalions of female warriors to fight along-side the men. The radicalism of Claire Lacombe and Pauline Léon led to the imprisonment of both in 1794. Female societies were finally banned, and women were denied political rights, actions contradicting the promises of the Declaration of Rights. Or perhaps not, for those promises dealt with the rights of *man and citizen*.[16]

It can even be argued, in light of the male resistance to women's effective participation in the French republic, that the symbolic use of the female image might be a compensation for their exclusion in reality. The argument is plausible, but it omits the fact that women were present at political demonstrations. As Eric Hobsbawm argues, women made up the majority in throngs protesting the scarcity of food, mainly because they were the ones most directly affected. They reappeared at the barricades of 1830, as attested by the valiant Marie Deschamps, immortalized by Delacroix. In 1848–51, there was the example of Madame Perrier, who, bearing the tricolor, led a republican column in Var. Whatever the disputes regarding its origin, the figure of Marianne surely pertains to a woman of the people who becomes involved in political struggles. The use of this allegory in France had a supporting basis; the signifier was not isolated from the signified.[17]

Among us Brazilians, if the male population was absent from the proclamation of the republic, what can be said of the female population? If there was not even a politically active male population in Brazil, how can one consider a political female population? There were, in fact, male political elites, who were called "public men." A "public woman," on the other hand, was a prostitute. Even in the Jacobin phase of the republic, during the Floriano administration, political participation was exclusively male. Not only did women not participate, but for them to do so was considered improper. Politics was a man's thing. The testimony of an eyewitness about the events of November 15 is revealing. Marshal Rondon relates in his memoirs that he left a party late that night without telling his girlfriend Chiquita what he was going to do. Despite being the orthodox positivist that he was, and thus a defender of the idea of woman's superiority over man, he held that politics was not part of the fair sex's realm.

A friend, unaware of events, passing by the General Headquarters as he took his daughters to the Normal School in the morning, was warned by an officer: "Where are you going, Xavier? This is no time to be out with your daughters."[18]

In considering politics outside a woman's field of action, Rondon was actually not departing from positivist orthodoxy. Despite his great emphasis on the female role and his declaration of the superiority of woman over man, Comte ultimately attributed to her the traditional role of wife, mother, and keeper of the home, for it was in these ways that women safeguarded the reproduction of the species and the moral health of humanity. Politics was a lesser task that fell to men. It was not by chance that the only women to emerge in the founding of the Brazilian republic were the daughters of Benjamin Constant. They appear in the classic role of women: sewing the first republican flag, which was conceived by the positivists and designed by Décio Villares.

Through closer observation, however, it may be possible to catch glimpses of women in the proclamation and the ensuing struggles. Rondon notes that when the troops left the barracks on the morning of November 15, several of the soldiers' wives followed for part of the way. In 1896, when the troops left for Canudos to supposedly defend the republic, various women such as wives or sutlers accompanied the expedition. In not one of these cases did female participation indicate support for the republic. Any such participation supported the opposite: in 1904, during the anti-vaccine revolt, newspapers registered the participation of prostitutes on the side of the rebels. Other sources also indicated the prostitutes' monarchical sympathies.[19] In this case, the representation of the republic as a prostitute was perhaps as insulting to them as it was to the new regime.

Gilberto Freyre has suggested some factors that favored the representation of the republic as a woman. One was the repudiation of the patriarchy of Pedro II, which had marked the country's political life for many years. Another was Catholic Mariolatry.[20] As for the former, there was the difficulty, mentioned earlier, of the existence of a female successor to the throne. At best, republican criticism could have neutralized this point only among the elite. As for the latter, there was without doubt Mariolatry in the country, and the positivists used it to insist on a feminine representation of humanity. But in this case, they sought to replace Mary with Clotilde. In France, Marianne could represent a respectable opposition to Mary. In Brazil, Clotilde did not even succeed in laying a hand on Mariolatry. The separation between church and state effected by the republic generated animosity among the populace, as the Canudos rebellion attests. The use of the Catholic symbol to represent the republic could smack of profanation.

As in France in the Second Empire, Mary was used as an antirepublican weapon in the Brazil of the First Republic. There was a deliberate effort by the bishops to promote the Marian cult, especially through Our Lady of Aparecida. Official pilgrimages began at the turn of the century. On September 8, 1904, Our Lady of Aparecida was crowned queen of Brazil. Note the date and the title: one day after the commemoration of Brazilian independence, a monarchical designation. There was no way to conceal the competition between the Catholic Church and the new regime for representation of the nation. The process reached its culmination in the decade of the 1930s. In 1930, Pius IX named Our Lady of Aparecida the patron saint of Brazil. The following year, Cardinal Dom Sebastião Leme, speaking before a crowd gathered in Rio de Janeiro, consecrated her as queen and patron saint of the country.

However problematic the capacity of Our Lady of Aparecida to represent the nation, it undoubtedly greatly surpassed that of any other feminine figure or even that of nearly all civic symbols. Besides putting down roots in the deep Catholic and Marian tradition, it offers the additional advantage of being Brazilian and black, quite opposite from the French, white Clotilde. Not even Princess Isabel could compete with Our Lady. The battle over the female allegory ended in a republican defeat, and further, in the defeat of the civic vis-à-vis the religious.[21]

THE ARTISTIC REPRESENTATION of women by Brazilian painters was a far cry from the women of the people. Virtually all of the painters passed through the Imperial Academy of Fine Arts, a fruit of the French Mission of 1816 and a bulwark of academic neo-classical painting. Beginning in the 1840s, the Academy instituted the prize of a trip to Europe. The emperor participated directly in support of the artists, financing periods of professional training in Europe from his own funds. Many of the best-known artists of the period spent years in Europe, mainly in France and Italy, at the expense of the government or the emperor. Some even extended their stay to ten years. Vítor Meireles spent eight years. Pedro Américo initially remained for five years and then later returned several times to execute works such as *The Battle of Avaí* and *Independence or Death*. He died in Florence. Rodolfo Amoedo, Belmiro de Almeida, Décio Villares, Antônio Parreiras, João Timóteo da Costa, Eliseu Visconti—all of these, from neoclassicists to romantics and impressionists, imbibed from European founts; in Europe, they produced a good part of their work.[22]

The figure of a woman, in the form of the portrait or in a historical or symbolic figure, was common in their artistic production. Their portraits were of the upper-class women who commissioned them. None were of mulatto, black, or Indian women. Not even Almeida Júnior (who, despite his training at the Academy and his stay in Europe, kept away from Rio and remained faithful to his rural traditions) produced portraits of women of the people. His most well-known feminine canvas, *The Model at Rest,* was painted in the best European style. The best black painter of the time, Estêvão da Silva, did not go to Europe, and he dedicated himself to painting still lifes.[23]

Indian women did appear in the painters' canvases. Vítor Meireles and Décio Villares painted Moema; José Maria de Medeiros, Lindóia and Iracema. Their very names reveal that they are not true Indians but images or romantic re-creations of the indigenous female. They are paintings inserted into the era's romantic Indianism. Yet even in this romantic vision, it did not occur to writers or painters to represent Brazil or the *patria* as an Indian woman. Brazil, under the empire, was indeed represented as a male Indian, as a reflection of romantic nativism. The Indian women of our painters had nothing to do with the nation. Was this because of the presence of a male monarch at the head of government or the patriarchism that dominated society? Was the empire—a centralizing, interventionist, and statist system—masculine? Was the female Brazil limited to the Catholic Church and the local churches? Questions remain.[24]

The majority of feminine representations at the time of the proclamation of the republic already bore the signs of a *fin-de-siècle*. The sensuality, beauty, and fragility of the woman were emphasized. It was the woman of urban Rio de Janeiro, if not Paris, turned into an object of consumption. It was no longer the woman as an agent or person, as could still be observed in portraits such as those by Décio Villares. If some "civic" women appeared, they came either from the Bible or from the history of other peoples. Pedro Américo painted Judith and Joan of Arc; he did not paint Joana Angélica or Anita Garibaldi. Perhaps the most representative canvas of the elegant woman, the *belle-époque* woman, is Belmiro de Almeida's *Dame à la rose* (fig. XI). Even the name is French. Woman as embodiment of sensuality touches the work of almost all the painters except the positivists, who did not paint nudes. Vítor Meireles had his Bacchante; Amoedo painted Salome and several nudes, some considered immoral by the critics of the time; Almeida Júnior created *The Model at Rest*. Let homage be paid here to Belmiro de Almeida, who, on deciding to paint a nude, did so using a model as seen from behind, her skin wrinkled and full of cellulite, a negation of the aesthetic feminine standards of the time. His canvas was rejected as immoral by a Paris salon.

Perhaps the most typical example of female sensuality is that of the painting *The Carioca Woman* (fig. XII) by Pedro Américo. A native of Paraíba who divided his life between the Brazilian court, Paris, and Florence, Pedro Américo painted battles on commission from the government, in addition to the heroines Joan of Arc and Judith. When it occurred to him to represent the Brazilian woman, he produced a nude and gave it the name of an inhabitant of the court. He could have entitled it *The Frenchwoman*. The canvas was painted in France during his first five-year stay in Europe. It was offered to Pedro II but returned because it did not meet palace standards of morality.

The woman depicted by the best painters of the period had no place in the world of politics and no place outside the home, unless it was in elegant salons and theaters or in the boutiques on Rua Ouvidor.[25] When she bordered on allegory—as in a biblical figure or an Indian maiden—the reference was not a civic one. There is no *Liberty* of Delacroix, or even *The Sabine Women* of David, in which the painter makes allegorical, political use of a classical theme. The question asked here is this: if they copied the Europeans in so many things, why couldn't Brazilian painters also copy the French tradition of representing the republic as a woman, whether or not there was a social base or a community of meaning for such a copy? Or, to go further, why, as artists, did they not free themselves of external conditioning and try to create a feminine allegory of the republic?

The answer may lie in the fact that the artists themselves were also far removed from the Brazilian republic. Despite the inevitable complaints of official protectionism that emerged in the final years of the monarchy, it remains true that the artistic world of the empire, largely concentrated in Rio de Janeiro, was dominated by imperial sponsorship through the intermediary of the Academy of Fine Arts and the personal role of the emperor. The republic attempted to innovate, but the generation of painters that represented it were formed in the imperial tradition. To this, add the lack of drama in its proclamation and the absence of popular throngs capable of arousing artistic inspiration.

The obstacles to the use of feminine allegory apparently could not be surmounted. The allegory fell short on two fronts: the signified, in which the republic proved far removed from the dreams of its idealizers; and the signifier, in which the civic woman, whether in reality or in artistic representation, did not exist. Under these circumstances, the only sensible way to utilize the allegory was to approximate a falsely considered republic to the vision of woman considered corrupt or perverse by society—namely, the prostitute. Ironically, the republic, or the "public thing," was ultimately allegorized by the public woman of the period, although such a woman, public in the civic sense, was perhaps a monarchist.

The allegory either dissolved from the lack of a community of imagination or fragmented into contradictory and inverted senses. One example of the dissolution emerged in 1902 in an episode at Flamengo Beach in Rio de Janeiro, as reported in *O Paiz*.[26] An attractive young woman appeared at the beach wearing a Phrygian cap. Her beauty and the unusualness of the cap attracted a large gathering of people. The girl was applauded, and there were huzzahs for the republic. The meaning of the huzzahs became clear when one young man observed that if the republic were like her, there would be no monarchists. Another bystander, no doubt referring to the well-known republican propagandist phrase of disappointment, sighed: "That's the republic of my dreams." There was no possible relation, not even allegorical, between the girl and the republic. The republic was neither beautiful nor desirable; it was neither freedom nor the nation. To the girl, the cap was merely an item of apparel or of fashion, not all that different from the swimsuit she was wearing. Surely, the onlookers wondered as they looked at her: Is she respectable (private) or public? A Mary or a *cocotte?* A Marianne, she was not.

chapter five

FLAG AND ANTHEM

The Weight of Tradition

The battle centering on republican symbolism also encompassed the flag and the anthem. Traditionally the most visible national symbols, these denote obligatory or quasi-obligatory usage and consideration. The struggle over the figure of the hero and over the use of feminine allegory in the myth of origin played an important part in legitimizing the new regime and was perhaps more revelatory, in the absence of legal exigency. But it was a struggle with a less conclusive outcome, for it did not decide the official symbolic representation of the republic. That battle lacked sharp boundaries, faced moving fronts, and had a vague time frame. In the case of the flag and the anthem, however, the battle was decisive. These two symbols were established legislatively at a specific time, and their adoption and use were compulsory.

It is no surprise, therefore, that the dispute centering on these two symbols was more intense than other disputes discussed so far, albeit of a shorter duration. It clearly reveals some of the cleavages among republicans and also enhances the earlier discussion of conditions that ease or impede manipulation of the collective imagination. In the case of the flag, the victory went to only one faction, the positivists, but this was largely due to incorporation in the new symbol of elements of the imperial tradition. In the case of the anthem, the victory of tradition was total: the old anthem remained. In spite of the republican leadership, it was the sole popular victory in the new regime.

The "Comet Brand" Flag

The unexpectedness of the events of November 15, 1889, left participants with no proper symbol to parade in the streets. The rebellious troops had no flag. A sergeant of the São Cristóvão Second Artillery Regiment threw away the imperial banner when the troops marched to the Santana field, but he had no replacement for it.[1] The republican movement, as a whole, had not adopted a flag of its own. For an anthem, it simply used the *Marseillaise*. It might be asked: if the *Marseillaise* was adopted, why not also the tricolor, the flag of the French Revolution and the French republics? The reason was that the *Marseillaise* was a symbol that transcended national borders and had become a universal symbol of revolution, whereas the tricolor retained its national characteristics. The *Marseillaise* stood for revolution and the radical republic; the tricolor stood for France.

Republicans were also aware that the tricolor, whose very origin was controversial, was an object of intense struggle in postrevolutionary France. Some said that it signified the union of the colors of Paris: red, blue, and white, the royal color. Others claimed that it represented the three estates: red for the nobility, white for the clergy, and blue for the third estate. Still others held that it was the creation of Lafayette, a commander of the National Guard who united the white of the Guard with the blue and red of the Parisian militias. Whatever the case, the tricolor was officially acclaimed at the Feast of Federation in 1790, when Paris adopted its colors. A virtual symbol of conciliation, it predated the French republic, as indicated in the argument that it represented the three estates. Perhaps this is why it survived the initial years of uncertainty, including the battle over its design and the position of the three colors. The tricolor was adopted officially by the National Convention in 1794, after being baptized in the blood of wars against invaders of the *patria*. David, the official painter of the French Revolution and friend of the Jacobins, designed the final version, placing the bands in a vertical position and the colors in their blue-white-red order.[2]

The Restoration abandoned the tricolor in favor of the white flag, which became the symbol of the monarchy and of reaction. But the tricolor was already a national symbol, and it was no accident that Louis Philippe decided to readopt it in 1830, after the fall of Charles X. In a scene laden with symbolism, he received it from the hands of Lafayette himself, who had sanctioned it in 1790. In 1848 the tricolor began to face new competition, this time not from the monarchical white flag but from the socialist red flag. Lamartine, a member of the revolutionary government, saved the tricolor by accusing the red flag of representing a party, not France. The commune adopted the red flag, but the Third Republic returned to the more traditional symbol. In 1880, at the first celebration of the 14th of July of the Third Republic, Paris decorated itself in blue, white, and red, as it did for the 1790 Feast of Federation. By now, the republic was France and the tricolor was its symbol; any of its revolutionary connotations were lost.

That Brazilian republicans encountered difficulties in adopting the tricolor, which was neither Brazilian nor revolutionary, is understandable. The choice of a flag left them divided and indecisive. To be sure, there were some attempts to create or adopt a new flag. First, there was the banner of the Inconfidentes, recognized by the various Tiradentes clubs formed within the country. There were also at least two versions inspired by the American model. One of them, in a rather impromptu manner, was raised by civilian republicans in the streets on November 15.

The story of that flag, considered the flag of the proclamation of the republic because it was raised by José do Patrocínio in the Municipal Chamber and remained there until November 19, illustrates the uncertainties of the republicans. It was a copy of the American flag. According to several statements, especially that of Captain Maximiano de Souza Barros, as reported in the newspaper *O Paiz* in November 1912, the flag was made by members of the Lopes Trovão

Republican Club for the reception of that republican leader on his return from Europe in 1888. In November 1889, it was stored at the Tiradentes Club, which met at the same location as the Lopes Trovão Club.[3] The flag retained the green and yellow colors of the imperial flag in its horizontal stripes. By the suggestion of the journalist Fávila Nunes, the quadrilateral had a black background to honor the black race. The stars were embroidered in white beads. The flag was made in a tailorshop that belonged to Captain Souza Barros himself. (See figs. XIII and XIV.)

The captain faced difficulties in explaining the choice of the American model. According to him, the club members were reluctant to accept the selection. Souza Barros admitted that the orientation of the revolutionaries, although they were enthusiastic about the United States, was completely French. They sang the *Marseillaise*— as they did on the very day of November 15—and looked only to France as a model. The captain hastened to assure them that the choice did not mean submission to American processes. In fact, the selection was somewhat surprising. In all likelihood, the club consisted of a majority of Jacobins and positivists, not São Paulo–style "democrats." The most logical option would have been an adaptation of the Inconfidentes' flag. One such adaptation was used at the first public commemoration of Tiradentes's death in 1881. In addition to the original design, the green and yellow colors of the imperial flag were added. It appeared for a long time in the *Gazeta da Noite*.[4] The decisive argument was probably resolved by the convenience of adopting an emblem that was also acceptable to both São Paulo and liberal republicans. In any case, it was the "American" flag that Patrocínio and others carried during the parade to the Municipal Chamber, where it was then hoisted.

A small but enthusiastic group of business employees, led by the photographer Augusto Malta, quickly put together another flag, mainly for personal use, copied from that of the Lopes Trovão Club. Contributing five mil-réis each, they bought material and made the flag. Later that same day, they paraded it down Ouvidor Street, circled the Largo do Paço, and shouted *vivas* to the republic, although somewhat fearfully since, according to Malta, it was still dangerous to express such sentiments on November 15.[5]

Apparently, in 1888, a naval officer stationed in Pernambuco, named Gabriel Cruz, independently made a flag inspired by the American model and sent it to Quintino Bocaiúva and José do Patrocínio. Cruz maintained the horizontal stripes in green and yellow, but in the quadrilateral he placed the Southern Cross on a blue background and encircled it with twenty stars. These stars, representing the states, were inspired by the imperial banner. It is not known what became of this flag.[6] Another flag in the American style (see fig. XV) was hoisted aboard the ship *Alagoas,* which took the royal family into exile. (It was lowered as the ship passed by São Vicente.) This flag, which Tobias Monteiro believed to be the one raised in the Chamber, was actually a copy; the ship departed before the first flag was removed from the Chamber. According to Tobias Monteiro's description, the quadrilateral was blue rather than black.[7] In all likelihood, it is the same flag that was formerly in the Naval Museum and can be found today in the Museum of the Republic. Malta provides no information about the color of this flag's quadrilateral. That of the *Alagoas* was blue, and years later, various witnesses to the events of November 15 would swear that the quadrilateral of the flag at the Lopes Trovão Club was also blue.[8] Today, that flag is housed in the Museum of the City of Rio de Janeiro; the color is black. Either the observers paid no attention to the color, or they decided to pay no attention to it. For those who copied this flag, the latter hypothesis is more likely. In such a case, there is still room for doubt: were they aware of the significance accorded the black color by the Lopes Trovão Club? On the question of such awareness hinges our knowing whether the colors were changed for aesthetic or racist reasons. Perhaps it was done for both reasons.

In any case, the orthodox positivists immediately reacted to the Lopes Trovão Club flag. They quickly conceived a different model, designed by Décio Villares, and sent it to the provisional government through the mediation of Benjamin Constant.[9] (See fig. XVI, as well as fig. XVII.) In the conception of the positivist flag, as in virtually everything, orthodox positivists followed the ideas of Comte. In his view, the initial phase of the organic transition of humanity would adapt the existing flags, to which the political motto "Order and Progress" would be added. Although the positivists conserved the green background, yellow lozenge, and blue sphere of the imperial flag, they removed from the calotte the imperial emblems: the cross, the armillary sphere, the crown, the coffee boughs and tobacco leaves. The stars encircling the sphere were relocated inside it. The main innovation—a highly controversial one that still encounters resistance—was the introduction of the motto "Order and Progress" in a band descending from left to right, representing the zodiac.

Rui Barbosa, a staunch liberal, must have sensed the difficulty in selling the idea of placing such a clearly positivist motto on the national flag. Not wishing to quarrel with his colleague Benjamin Constant, who was the true ideologue of the republic among the military, he accepted the idea but asked Teixeira Mendes to publicly justify the new emblem. The provisional government's decree adopting the positivist flag came out on November 19, only four days after the proclamation, a feat that demonstrated the efficiency of the orthodox wing. Teixeira Mendes's justification was published in the *Diário Oficial* of November 24; it began a controversy that would involve the two principal apostles of orthodoxy, Mendes himself and Miguel Lemos, until the end of their days.[10]

In his initial defense, Teixeira Mendes did not mention the flag that circulated on November 15. He merely justified the new flag.[11] Constant, in keeping with positivist principles, suggested that the national emblem be symbolic of brotherhood and that it link the past to the present and the future. The tie to the past lay in preserving part of the imperial flag, credited by Mendes as the work of José Bonifácio. (It was actually designed by a disciple of David, Jean-Baptiste Debret, who also painted the French tricolor.) The imperial design and colors, representations of Brazil's nature and riches, were preserved. Even the cross remained: the Southern Cross, a lay cross, was looked upon sympathetically by Catholics. In this way, the past and tradition, both political and religious, were recognized; although monarchy and Catholicism were phases of mankind's evolution to be surpassed, they were also necessary bearers of positive aspects.

The flag, Teixeira Mendes continued, must also represent the present, the new regime, and the future. The motto "Order and Progress" fulfilled this requirement. As a consequence of the scientific discoveries of the Master's social dynamic, he stated, a world hitherto divided between the two tendencies, with excesses of progress replacing excesses of order, was transitioning toward a unified conception. According to Teixeira Mendes, now all Brazilian people would aspire to conciliation. He went on to describe the placement of the star and the choice of constellations. Finally, in a true tour de force, he attempted to link the flag's green color to an affiliation with France, "the center of the West," thus tying it to "all past human evolution, into the most remote future." The green represented the hope and peace initiated by the French Revolution. Those who stormed the Bastille carried green leaves, torn from trees of the royal palace, as emblems. The flag also recalled Tiradentes, whose rebellion was betrayed in the same year as the French Revolution.

Opposition to the new flag arose immediately. The *Diário do Commercio* on November 24 accused the government of adopting a symbol that, because it lent itself to ridicule and reflected the position of a religious sect, was unsuitable as a national symbol. Teixeira Mendes replied to this criticism through an irritated and dogmatic article in the *Diário Oficial* of November 26.[12] He insisted that the motto "Order and Progress" did not imply allegiance to positivism but rather dealt with a universal aspiration, an aspiration of all Brazilians. Could the journalist who criticized the motto really state that Brazil's people did not desire order and progress? Comte, like other geniuses—Aristotle, Confucius, Descartes, and so forth—merely encapsulated the aspiration of his time. Furthermore, the positivist "sect" desired nothing from the republic, not even political appointments. It simply wanted the ruling republican dictatorship to guarantee order and progress. Finally, Mendes justified the introduction of the caption: images are more effective when accompanied by words. The Inconfidentes' banner also bore a slogan ("Freedom, albeit late"), but it was not adopted because it did not fit in with the new times; freedom was no longer an end in itself but a condition for order and progress. That flag was rendered, so to speak, behind the times.

The layout of the stars also faced the criticisms that it was scientifically incorrect and that the new regime intended to take the revolution even to the heavens and astronomy. After consulting a European astronomer, a journalist sent an article from Paris to the *Gazeta de Notícias* that argued that the constellations were upside down, that the dimensions of the Southern Cross were exaggerated, and that the position of several stars was incorrect.[13] Teixeira Mendes returned to the fray in a publication of the positivist Apostolate on June 3, 1890.[14] He accused the *Gazeta's* journalist of being unpatriotic because the journalist ridiculed a national symbol! He then went on to play an ambiguous game. On one hand, he cited the opinion of astronomer Manuel Pereira Reis, the scientific consultant for the new flag, that the layout of the stars reflected the view of the sky from Rio de Janeiro on the morning of November 15, 1889. On the other hand, especially in light of the obvious errors, he argued that the flag was an idealization, a symbol, and an emblem that could not be subjected to an unyielding, representational model of reality. Whether or not the position of the stars was correct, it did recall the Brazilian sky, unlike the stars of the imperial flag and the stars of the American flag in relation to the heavens. Here, the emblematizing of the stars fulfills the essential purpose of the flag: to reach the hearts of Brazilians.

Also in 1890, Eduardo Prado, an irreconcilable enemy of the new regime, published a book entitled *A bandeira nacional* (The National Flag). Among other criticisms, he emphasized the astronomical inaccuracy of the layout of the constellations.[15] Prado went into great detail to point out the mistake. In the years that followed, the struggle over the national flag became more aggressive, especially during the Jacobin period. All indications suggest that Deodoro himself was dissatisfied with the new flag. After Benjamin Constant's death, it is said that when Deodoro attempted to change the flag, he again provoked the wrath of Teixeira Mendes, who threatened Deodoro with the ghost of Constant. According to Mendes, Constant was the true founder of the republic and the guarantor against metaphysical, clerical, and Sebastianist reactions.

Not even Floriano Peixoto was free from positivist vigilance. On September 7, 1892, a particular incident shook Rio de Janeiro. A Portuguese merchant on Rua da Assembléia, undoubtedly a monarchist, displayed a signboard depicting the positivist flag on which the motto "Order and Progress" was replaced by what the *Diário de Notícias* termed a "defaming inscription." The inscription was unspecified, but it was probably "Comet Brand," a name opponents gave the new flag because it resembled advertisements of a wine by that name. In addition, the motto-bearing band was confused with a comet's tail. In Coelho Neto's 1929 novel *Fogo fátuo,* a character refers to the "Comet Brand" flag only a few days after the proclamation.[16] In any case, on that September 7, the anniversary of Brazilian independence, some people who were offended by the merchant's irreverence invaded the store, tore out all of the signboards, and formed a procession to take the national banner to the Itamaraty, then the presidential palace, amid cheers for the republic and for President Peixoto. At the palace, there were heated speeches in front of a small crowd. A commission handed over the flag to the presidential guard. Peixoto, as was customary, offered some ambiguous message about defending the national banner, one that everyone interpreted as a clear-cut stance against its modification. Miguel Lemos lost no time: on September 9, he telegraphed the state governors to indicate that the president was against the change.

With the president's nod, Deputy Valadão, a military man close to Peixoto and involved with a bill to change the flag, quickly wired the governors and denied Lemos's interpretation. Some positivist governors spoke out. Students at the War College launched a virulent manifesto, in the name of Benjamin Constant, against the idea of changing the flag. The manifesto was positivist, anti-politician, and deeply authoritarian. The reason for the reaction against the flag, it argued, was clear: it intended to profane the memory of Constant, "disguising, by means of an empirical and servile imitation, the true historical tie of our nationality." Read: those advocating change

wanted to adopt the model of the American flag; they wanted a liberal democratic republic instead of the republican dictatorship espoused by positivism and linked to French political traditions. The
manifesto also spoke of "indecent, corrupting, and petty politics" and
the "parliamentary games of our charlatan politicians." In short, the
manifesto denied that congress and the head of government had the
authority to modify the flag. Only Constant, the leader of the November 15 revolution, had the appropriate representative standing to
institute the flag, the symbol coalescing the collective aspirations of
that moment. The Republican Club of Rio Grande do Sul, another
positivist stronghold, voiced a similar opinion.[17]

The bill presented to congress by Valadão and other deputies intended to remove the positivist motto from the flag and replace the
stars with the coat of arms of the republic. Valadão telephoned the
governors to ask their opinion prior to the September 7 episode. He
publicly stated that Peixoto favored the change. After the manifesto
issued by students at the War College, he consulted battalion com-
manders and garrison superior officers about the matter. The reply,
according to Miguel Lemos, was against modification. The Chamber
of Deputies decided that state legislatures and municipal authorities
should be consulted regarding the removal of a "symbol of any sect"
from the flag. Apparently, however, the consultation never occurred,
and the Chamber, upon resuming its duties, did not return to the
subject. An incident worth noting was the bishop of Rio de Janeiro's
refusal to bless the new flag when requested to do so by a commander
of the National Guard. The reason given pertained to one of the
flag's elements: the motto of the religious positivist sect.[18]

The action of the orthodox positivists was extremely clever and
effective. Despite being a minority, they succeeded in mobilizing the
Jacobin groups, especially the military radicals. The veto of these
groups blocked the change. Peixoto, although opposed to the flag—
he was no positivist—looked to them as his bases of support. He
shared many of their prejudices, especially their aversion to politicians and congress. Hence, he could not openly confront them over
such a delicate matter. A commission from the War College even
personally visited him to protest against the change. At the end of

1893, the outbreak of civil war made his situation even more precarious, and the flag issue died. The positivists still scorned Peixoto's memory, erecting a monument to him in which the main part was called *Sentinel of the Flag*. The marshal appears bareheaded out of respect for the banner and holds a sword in his right hand, ready for battle. Behind him is an enormous flag with the figures of Tiradentes, José Bonifácio, and Benjamin Constant; the motto "Order and Progress" is clearly visible.

Despite the resistance to the positivist motto, which lingers even today, the republican flag had greater acceptance than the created myths of the November 15 heroes, and it certainly aroused greater respect than the feminine depiction of the republic. Cartoonists quickly adopted the flag in their allegorical representations of the new regime. However, a political cartoon by Pereira Neto in the *Revista Illustrada* of November 16, 1889, constitutes an enigma. It portrayed the new regime's first representation of the republic in the form of a woman.

Modeled on Athena in her warrior version, as indicated by the sword and shield, the female figure in Pereira Neto's cartoon does not depart from the previously examined stereotype. What is surprising is the flag she holds in her left hand. It is, without a doubt, the new flag: one can see the blue lozenge bisected by the zodiac's band that descends from left to right. The problem, however, lies in the date: How was it possible to publish such a cartoon on the day after the proclamation? Alvarus suggests that the magazine was already in press, as if awaiting the event.[19] But this does not resolve the question of the flag's presence. According to the positivists, it was only after seeing the "American" flag on November 15 that they mobilized to present another model. There was, therefore, the task of conceiving it, consulting the astronomer Pereira Reis, and calling on Décio Villares to design it. In addition, according to Teixeira Mendes, his first suggestion to the provisional government (read Benjamin Constant) was to adopt the flag proposed by Comte for the third phase of the organic transition: a green background edged by the colors of each nationality. Miguel Lemos reminded him that Brazil was still in the first phase and that the new emblem should preserve that of the

GLORIA Á PATRIA! HONRA AOS HEROES DO DIA 15 DE NOVEMBRO DE 1889.

HOMENAGEM DA "REVISTA ILLUSTRADA"

28. Pereira Neto, "Glory to the Patria!"
Revista Illustrada, November 16, 1889.

empire and include the motto. Only then was the new flag designed. In the account of Constant's meeting with the positivists on November 17, the flag is unmentioned, although there is a reference to the introduction of the motto. Was the new model already decided upon? If this were the case, Teixeira Mendes should have already spoken with Constant about the matter on November 15, in his meeting with members of the provisional government.[20] But at that moment, he clearly did not speak with Miguel Lemos, and, if he suggested a flag, it was that of the transition's third phase, not the one finally adopted.

A puzzling element remains: the political cartoon of November 16. The figure of Deodoro da Fonseca, holding his cap, in a pose almost identical to that of Bernardelli's painting clearly indicates that the cartoon was drawn after the proclamation, but no later than on the 15th itself in order to allow for printing and distribution on the 16th. How, then, could it contain the new flag? The mystery becomes more intricate if we recall that *O Mequetrefe* of November 17 portrays both an allegorical female of the republic and José do Patrocínio, who is grasping the "American" flag he raised up in the Municipal Chamber.

How are we to resolve this? Was it mere coincidence? Might Pereira Neto have taken the imperial flag, eliminated the symbols of the old regime, and placed the Southern Cross (also a well-known symbol—there was an Order of the Southern Cross) inside the sphere? It is curious that the motto "Order and Progress" is not found in his flag. But why then the zodiacal band, exactly as it was in the positivist banner? Another possibility is that the magazine did not circulate on the 16th, its date of publication, but rather one or two days later, thus giving the cartoonist enough time to contact the positivists, although in the end he rejected their motto.

In any case, beginning in December 1889, cartoonists systematically used the new flag with the motto. The *Revista Illustrada* again showed it, with the motto, in the issue for June 21, 1890, which hails the recognition of the Brazilian republic by the French one. Despite a susceptibility to ridicule, as the label "Comet Brand" attests, and despite the rise of various savage criticisms of using a woman to

represent the republic, the new flag symbol was spared. One reason
for its survival was perhaps the fear of reprisals. But such fear was
more realistic at the beginning of the new regime, especially in the
Jacobin phase. That fear was no longer justified after the 1904 defeat
of the positivists in the military at the beginning of the Rodrigues
Alves administration. It can be supposed that the flag was respected
and accepted either because it was the official symbol or because it
possessed legitimacy in some other way. One of the few examples reflecting the alterations in the motto is a political cartoon, of a more
critical than mocking tone, by Angelo Agostini in *D. Quixote* for
November 25, 1895. The republic appears as a woman riding back-
ward in a direction opposite that of progress, in contrast to the
United States and the other Hispanic American republics. Instead of
"Order and Progress," the banner bears the inscription "Disorder and
Retrogression." One of the reasons for that retrogression is clearly
expressed in the banner borne by Prudente de Morais, which reads
"Positivist Politics."

The flag appears less frequently in architecture and in paintings.
Positivist monuments, as we have seen, always have it positioned
prominently; it represents both the *patria* and the republic. It envel-
ops the figures of Benjamin Constant and Floriano Peixoto in their
monuments in Rio de Janeiro. In the monument to Júlio de Castilhos, it dominates the principal frame at the front of the pyramid. In
the area of painting, there is the canvas by Pedro Bruno (Fig. XVIII),
which is perhaps the most important one regarding the flag theme. It
was only completed in 1919, later than other works, so perhaps it
sought to reconcile the positions that contended at the outset of the
Brazilian republic. The painting clearly exhibits positivist characteristics. Although its object is the flag, the painting's title is *A Pátria*, a
title favored by the orthodox wing. Miguel Lemos may have endorsed the content: a group of women of all ages—daughters, mothers, grandmothers—sewing the flag. It exalts the flag, the *patria,* and
women's moral roles in raising their children and in honoring the
moral values of family and fatherland. The maternal symbolism is
also obvious in the nursing mother and in the woman who is embracing and kissing a child. The masculine presence is limited to an

29. "The French Republic,"
Revista Illustrada, June 21, 1890.

30. Angelo Agostini, "The Year 1896,"
D. Quixote, November 25, 1895.

old man, nearly hidden from view, in the right-hand corner. The
painting probably refers to the positivist flag sewn by Benjamin Constant's daughters and offered to the Military School. Included in the
painting, as another positivist vestige, is a portrait of Tiradentes
hanging on the wall.

On the other hand, the canvas also includes nonpositivist elements. First of all, there is the portrait of Deodoro da Fonseca, which
would never be acceptable to orthodox positivists, especially in the
absence of Benjamin Constant. Second, as in the *Revista Illustrada*
flag of November 16, the motto "Order and Progress" does not appear. The artist, by cleverly depicting an incomplete flag, includes
the white band but excludes the motto. Finally, an image of Our
Lady is on a table, signaling a clear preference for the Catholic symbol over the positivist one of Clotilde. The painting, which won its
creator a trip to Europe, accurately represents several reasons for the

A PRIMEIRA NOTICIA.

Ao chegar a primeira noticia da entrega de Montevidéo, o povo, justamente enthusiasmado, rodeou o carro do Imperador. Sua Magestade, commovido ante essa prova de amor, correspondeu affectuosamente à manifestação popular.

31. H. Fleiuss, "The First News,"
Semana Illustrada, March 12, 1865.

relative success of the new flag. Through the flag and in the figure of Tiradentes, it emphasizes the ties with the past; through the figure of the Catholic Virgin, it reflects the prevailing popular culture; and through the figure of Deodoro, it reconciles the republican factions. The banner did not break with the cultural and civic tradition of the country, as the orthodox positivists wished. The yellow lozenge on the green background fluttered on warships and battlefields during the Paraguayan War. In Rio de Janeiro, news of victory was commemorated by the people who paraded the national colors in the streets, as attested abundantly by the cartoons of Henrique Fleiuss in the *Semana Illustrada.* The flag was flown for nearly a century of the country's independent life and was immortalized in the fiery verses of republican poet Castro Alves. The republican flag was still the "green and yellow banner," despite the label "Comet Brand."

The "Ta-ra-ta-ta-tchin": Victory of the People

The battle over the national anthem, more than that over the flag, signified a victory for tradition. One could even call it a popular victory, perhaps the sole victorious intervention by the people since the establishment of the new regime.

The propaganda-minded republicans had no anthem of their own. Their anthem was the *Marseillaise,* which, as Medeiros e Albuquerque attests, was sung at every demonstration.[21] The 14th of July was a headache for the French representative in Rio de Janeiro: republicans, taking advantage of the date, would openly sing the revolutionary hymn and fight the monarchy. The diplomat faced the dilemma of either risking conflict with the government by celebrating the date or displeasing his compatriots by not doing so.[22]

Such cases clearly reflected the ambiguity of the French anthem. Until the end of the nineteenth century, the *Marseillaise* was both the French anthem and the anthem of revolutionaries in all countries. In France, it had a troubled career. It was composed in April 1792 by Rouget de Lisle as the "war cry for the army of the Rhine," even before the proclamation of the republic, when France had just declared war on the king of Hungary and Bohemia. It spread rapidly, competing with other popular patriotic songs such as *Ça ira* and *La carmagnole.*[23] In July 1792, when the Marseille *fédérés* left for Paris, each carried a copy of the song; they sang it en route and on their arrival in Paris. They especially sang it on August 10, when they helped to invade the Tuileries, depose the monarch, and proclaim the republic. The name of the song was widely accepted: it was the song of the people of Marseilles, the *Marseillaise.* A warrior composition par excellence, it was taken onto the fields of battle, arousing enthusiasm wherever it was heard. One general wrote to his government: "Send me a thousand men or a printing of the *Marseillaise.*"[24]

The National Convention adopted the *Marseillaise* as the national anthem of the republic in 1794. From that date onward, it had a turbulent history, suffering the caprice of political ups and downs. Suspiciously looked upon by the Napoleonic Empire and rejected

32. Pils, *Rouget de Lisle Sings the Marseillaise*
for the Prefect of Strasbourg.

during the Restoration, it made a triumphant return at the barricades of 1830. Delacroix's Liberty sings it as she leads the people into battle. The song also explodes from the throat of Victory in Rudé's sculpture. But under Louis Philippe's government, it became subversive once again. In 1848 it reappeared at the barricades and was sung during the Second Republic. The following year, Pils painted his famous, though historically inaccurate, canvas in which he represented Rouget de Lisle singing his composition for the prefect of Strasbourg. In the Second Empire, it returned to a clandestine standing, only to be rehabilitated during the Franco-Prussian War of 1870 and the Paris Commune.

It was not until 1879 that Gambetta restored it to the level of a national anthem. He sought to reduce its bellicose, revolutionary aspect so as to adapt it to the political conditions of the Third Republic. As Michel Vovelle notes, this officialization signified a displacement of sentiment, a domestication of the old war cry. In 1882, the president of the Council stated that the *Marseillaise* was not a war song and that the republic was a government of concord and tolerance.[25] Beginning with the turn of the century, it found itself challenged in popularity among the working class by the *Internationale,* which was composed in 1888.

Aside from the attempts in France to make the *Marseillaise* the anthem of the nation rather than of revolution, it still represented a cry of war and revolt in other countries. Hence the difficulties faced by the French representative in Rio de Janeiro. To Brazilian republicans, it was the very spirit of revolution. However, they needed to provide a Brazilian touch to the movement. At a spiritist session in Rio,[26] the spirit of Rouget de Lisle dictated the music and lyrics for a *Brazilian Marseillaise.* The lyrics were atrocious:

> .... Free being!
> Made free
> Let our breast cry out!
> Let our breast cry out!
> Like broken thunder!
> Long live, long live, long live the military,
> Strong, loyal!
> Long live, long live the military![27]

Silva Jardim sought Brazilian lyrics for the *Marseillaise* at the end of 1888 and the beginning of 1889. But Olavo Bilac and Luís Murat, whom he approached, refused to cooperate because of the influence of José do Patrocínio, who was then at the height of his Isabelist, or monarchist, phase. Medeiros e Albuquerque thereupon offered to write the lyrics; sung to the melody of the *Marseillaise,* they were adopted as the official anthem of the Republican Party. A short time before the proclamation, a contest to put music to the text was won by Ernesto de Souza, a pharmacist.[28]

On November 15, however, the *Marseillaise* in the music and lyrics by Rouget de Lisle was still heard in the streets. On November 22, 1889, the provisional government decided to sponsor another competition to put Medeiros e Albuquerque's lyrics to music. In the meantime, an episode occurred that altered the course of events. Major Serzedelo Correia had prepared a military manifesto to Deodoro da Fonseca on January 15, 1890, with the undeclared goal of promoting the members of the provisional government by acclamation. Citizens and naval troops gathered in front of the Itamaraty palace. Deodoro was proclaimed generalissimo; Wandenkolk, vice admiral; and Minister of War Benjamin Constant, brigadier general. Bands played the *Marseillaise* and military marches, but they could not arouse the enthusiasm of the small crowd gathered in front of the palace. An air of expectation was created. It is not known if what followed was planned or spontaneous, but some people requested that the bands play the old national anthem by Francisco Manuel da Silva. Serzedelo took this appeal to Constant, who consulted Deodoro. They decided on the spot that the bands would play the anthem and that it would remain the national anthem. The military bands, as if expecting the result, burst forth with the popular *Ta-ra-ta-ta-tchin*. According to eyewitness accounts, the audience was delighted. Some wept upon hearing, once again, the chords of the old anthem. It was undoubtedly held dear by the soldiers who fought in Paraguay to the sounds of its lively, happy notes. After the ceremony, the bands, accompanied by the populace, departed through the streets, playing the anthem.[29]

There is no record of any negative reaction to the decision to retain the monarchy's anthem. If there was some maneuvering on Serzedelo's part, it undoubtedly corresponded to the wishes of the people and to a large part of the military, especially the Navy, which had never been enthusiastic about the republic. Journalists linked to the government had already insisted on the necessity of retaining the anthem. They recalled that Francisco Manuel's music had taken root in popular tradition and had become a symbol of the nation rather than of a political regime. Raul Pompéia shared this opinion. He did not believe in commissioned anthems, for they typically lacked ties to the joys and despair of a people.[30]

In addition to its popular acclamation, Francisco Manuel's music was ratified in elite circles by a derivative piece: a fantasia by Louis

Moreau Gottschalk. The New Orleans pianist arrived in Rio in May 1869, after a long journey through South America. Preceded by his fame as a virtuoso pianist and his recognition in Europe, where he had studied for eleven years, Gottschalk was received with honors by the emperor. His concerts created what he called a furor in the court. He quickly composed a fantasia based on the national anthem, which he executed, to the delight of audiences, at all his performances. To better understand this public reaction, we must remember that the Paraguayan War was in its final year, and patriotic spirits were particularly aroused.

Gottschalk, a Fitzcarraldo *avant la lettre,* planned a gigantic concert with 650 musicians and nine National Guard bands—four from the Navy, two from the Army, and one made up of music teachers. There were 55 strings, 65 clarinets, 60 trumpets, 60 trombones, 55 saxhorns, 50 tubas, 11 piccolos, and more. The city had never seen anything like it. The pianist exhausted himself in the effort of rehearsing this multitude: "I'm a symphonic battery; a steam engine that became a man. . . . My heart is a volcano; my head, chaos!" he wrote to friends. The premiere was on November 24. It was, as one reporter put it, held in an atmosphere like that of the Arabian Nights. After several works by Gottschalk and other composers, the program ended with a *Solemn Brazilian March,* a fantasia based on the national anthem and accompanied by a cannon salvo behind the scenes. The march was an apotheosis, which had to be repeated. The next day, Gottschalk almost fainted from exhaustion on stage and had to be taken home. He never recovered. His death on December 18 occasioned mourning throughout the city. He was a musical meteor that had passed through Rio de Janeiro, leaving in its wake, among other remembrances, the acclamation of Francisco Manuel da Silva's anthem.[31]

The government contest was transformed into a competition to choose music for an anthem of the proclamation of the republic, not the national anthem. The decision was announced on January 20, 1890, at the Teatro Lírico, in the presence of members of the provisional government and an audience that completely filled the hall. Some of the most important musicians of the time, such as Francisco

Braga, Jerônimo de Queiroz, Alberto Nepomuceno, and Leopoldo Miguez, competed for the honor. The latter was director of the National Institute of Music. According to Medeiros e Albuquerque, Rodrigues Barbosa, an employee of the Ministry of the Interior and collaborator with Miguez in the reorganization of the Institute, arranged for a claque to applaud the director's music: he packed the theater with Miguez's friends. This effort was offset in part by students from the Professional Institute, where Francisco Braga taught. Learning of the trick, they decided to play Miguez's anthem atrociously. The two compositions by Braga and Miguez were the favorites. The jury awarded the victory to Miguez, whose composition had a measure from the *Marseillaise* in its opening phrase. The government then declared that Miguez's music be called the *Anthem of the Proclamation of the Republic* (for those who do not recall it: "Liberty, liberty! Spread your wings over us!"). When the winning anthem was played again, the public asked for the old anthem, which was now, once more, the national anthem. According to an impartial reporter of *O Paiz,* "The impression that Francisco Manuel's composition made on the public is indescribable. It was delirium! If it had not been chosen on the 15th of this month, the national anthem of the United States of Brazil would have been acclaimed yesterday."[32]

There was no way to attempt to change the music of the old anthem without incurring great displeasure and possibly popular resistance. The Brazilian republic won by yielding to tradition. Francisco Manuel's anthem was given new lyrics by Osório Duque Estrada, since the original lyrics had fallen into disuse, even under the monarchy.

The later history of the republic confirmed the popular roots of the imperial anthem, and with its new lyrics, it became popularized as the *Virundum*. In times of opposition to military governments, the anthem often served as a channel for the outpouring of the crowd's civic emotion in the public square. Nothing more can be asked of a national symbol than this: the capacity to translate collective sentiment and to express the civic emotion of the members of a national community.

33. "Anthem of the Proclamation of the Republic of
the United States of Brazil," National Library.

The two episodes related here reinforce the earlier analyses of
the hero and of feminine representation. The Brazilian republic, unlike either its French or American models, lacked sufficient popular
backing to remake the national collective imagination. Its roots were
shallow; they ran deep only in narrow sectors of the population,
mainly among the educated and urban population. The bulk of the
nation was aloof, if not hostile, to it. The proclamation of the republic through the initiative of the military also did nothing to contribute to its popularization. The effort to re-create the collective
imagination fell into the void, where it did not encounter resistance
or lend itself to ridicule.

Only when the new republic turned to deeper cultural traditions,
which at times were alien to its image, did it somewhat succeed in
popularizing itself: to independence and to religion, in the case of
Tiradentes; to monarchical symbols, in the case of the flag; to the

civic tradition, in the case of the anthem. Republicans frequently complained about the inability of the new government to generate enthusiasm. In May 1890, one of them wrote to the *Revista Illustrada* to complain that there was still no republican coin six months after the proclamation; that neither the *Marseillaise* nor the proclamation anthem was heard; and that the new flag was seldom seen. Monarchical symbolism endured, appearing in almost all public buildings. The writer appealed to the government to make a greater effort to awaken people's enthusiasm by using these powerful means of propaganda.[33]

chapter six

POSITIVISTS AND THE MANIPULATION OF THE COLLECTIVE IMAGINATION

The constant presence of the orthodox positivists is clearly evident in the preceding chapters. They involved themselves intensely in all of the symbolic battles discussed here: the origin of myth, the hero, the feminine allegory, and the flag. Only in the case of the anthem do they fail to appear, perhaps because they agreed with the solution adopted. They constituted the most active and most belligerent group with respect to attempts to transform the republic into a regime that would not only be accepted but also be loved by the populace. Their weapons were the written word and civic symbols; through and with these, they fought with an apostolic dedication (or, as their enemies would say, with fanatical obsession), thus warranting special attention.

At least two points can help us understand their actions. The first and more obvious is Comtean doctrine itself; the second is their conception of the political tactics that should be adopted in Brazil to promote the reforms indicated by Comte. I shall begin with the first.

The Comtean View

Even before 1844, when Comte met Clotilde de Vaux (see fig. XIX), the person responsible for his "moral regeneration," his thinking already displayed elements that did not originate from scientific or positivistic sources, in the strict meaning of these terms. The influence of Henri de Saint-Simon's utopian thought on Comte must not have been alien to this tendency, which manifested itself principally in Comte's grandiose visions about the evolution of humanity and, perhaps, in the desire to replace the Catholic utopia of the Middle Ages with the lay utopia of the Positivist Age.[1]

But, most importantly, it was after meeting Clotilde de Vaux that Comte developed the utopian and religious elements of his thinking. Feeling was placed in the forefront, while reason, the basis of his earlier work, was relegated to a subordinate position. Instead of a simple philosophy or a philosophy of history, Comtean positivism evolved toward a religion of humanity in its theology, its rituals, and its hagiography. In seeking to be a "lay" conception, it merged the religious with the civic, or, rather, the civic became religious. Great men of humankind became the saints of the new religion; civic celebrations were its rituals; the Comtean philosophy and its political ideas became its theology; positivists were the new priests. Comte placed the sentiment of altruism, his replacement for Catholic charity, at the base of the new humanity. Still following the model of Catholic communitarianism, he emphasized institutions or concepts of solidarity and ranked them in a hierarchy. The family remained the base, followed by the fatherland, and then, as the culmination of the process, humanity.[2]

The "Clotildean turn" was clear in Comte's later vision of women and their role in social evolution. In his earlier *Cours de philosophie,* his position on women followed the traditional view of their inferiority to men. In later years, after mixing discoveries in biology and Catholic-feudal views, he affirmed the social and moral superiority of women over men. Such superiority was based on the claim that women represented the affective and altruistic side of human nature, while men represented the active and selfish side. Women, as biology demonstrated, had the principal responsibility for the reproduction of the species, while men were more suitable for transforming the environment and for industrial activity. In the preservation of the species, women's role was not limited to reproduction but was also critical to the family, in which, as mothers, they were responsible for shaping the moral upbringing of future citizens.

Hence, the allegorical representation of the feminine figure was merely a step in this direction. The Catholic Virgin, allegory of the Catholic Church, became the Positivist Virgin-Mother, allegory of humanity. As Comte himself stated, "Worship of the Virgin-Mother by the West [became] unconsciously a preamble to the worship of Humanity. For the Great Being is a realization of the feminine utopia in that it needs no external agency for its fecundation."[3] The feminine utopia, in this case, would be parthenogenesis, or the capacity for women to generate children without male intervention, an evolution that Comte believed he could deduce from the advances in biological knowledge of his era. The next step for him was to specify the type of woman who should represent humanity and to express his wish that the figure of Clotilde be stamped on Western flags.

The dogma of the superiority of feeling and love over reason and action also applied to races and cultures. The black race would be superior to the white because, like women in contrast to men, it was characterized by the predominance of feeling, while the white race was marked by reason. Latin countries held the same advantageous position in relation to Anglo-Saxon countries. They represented the feminine side of humanity and were the bearers of moral progress, while the Anglo-Saxons represented the masculine side, material progress, and the less noble sciences. Despite the great importance of material progress, its role was secondary in the evolution of humanity, which was principally based on morality and the expansion of altruism. Comte believed that among the Latin countries, France was *le pays central* and Paris the central city. Positivist temples should be built facing Paris, just as Muslim mosques faced Mecca.

In Comte's thought, the republic was the essential factor in the organic transition to the final phase of humanity. It would initiate

34. Décio Villares, *Humanity Personified*
in Clotilde de Vaux.

the transition by overcoming the metaphysical phase, in which external elements (hereditary monarchies based on the divine right of kings) still hindered human evolution. Republics should be true communities, extensions of the family. Comte, following Rousseau's model, advocated republics that did not exceed three million inhabitants and that were approximately the size of Belgium. France should be divided into seventeen different republics. In the final phase, the world would have some five hundred different republics. These would be the "normal fatherlands," though the philosopher preferred to call them "motherlands," in order to emphasize the communitarian and affective aspects while simultaneously recalling the feminine collective imagination. From all of this stemmed the idea of representing the republican *patria* through the figure of a woman.

Having distanced himself from Saint-Simon because of that philosopher's tendency to create a parody of Catholicism, Comte ended up doing exactly the same. Volume 4 of his *Système de politique*

35. Eduardo de Sá,
*Humanity Personified in
Clotilde de Vaux.*

positive is devoted to descriptions of the new rites of worship. Comte provides a positivist calendar, with thirteen months, each month with four weeks, and each week with seven days. Each month and each day are dedicated to a figure considered important in the evolution of humanity. There is also a "sociolatrous [*sociolátrico*] framework," in which are prescribed eighty-one civic celebrations, including one dedicated to women. The positivist temple should display the statue of humanity in a central position and include side altars, one of them dedicated to female saints.

As a result of these ideas, Comte attributed great importance to feelings and to the means of reaching the feelings, that is, to artistic expression. Aesthetics was another area developed by Comte after the Clotildean "rebirth." In the first volume of the *Système*, in a chapter entitled "Aesthetic Aptitude of Positivism," he proposed a general theory of art. According to positivist aesthetics, the artistic imagination must have feeling as its inspiration, reason as its base, and action as its end. This means that it cannot remove itself from the reality defined by science, just as it should try to have an impact on politics through the idealization of the values and the individuals considered models for humanity. In his own words, "Art consists always of an ideal representation of that which is; it is destined to cultivate our instinct of perfection."[4] This is a naturalistic aesthetic, in which the beautiful is subordinated to a notion of truth and places itself at the service of good. As I have already observed, it is a conception of art not far removed from that of David, if we leave aside questions of style. The neoclassical revolutionary style could make way for the romantic, without changing the view of nature and the purpose of art.

The Bolshevik Tactics of the Orthodox Positivists

Brazilian orthodox positivists generally followed the final teachings of Comte, emphasizing their religious and ritualistic aspects.[5] For this reason, opponents accused them of an excess of orthodoxy, religious fanaticism, and even insanity. More than anything else, they ridiculed the positivists' Clotildolatry.[6] What their adversaries sometimes failed to understand was that their orthodoxy, rather than being an end in itself, had a political goal. And it was precisely for the sake of this goal, on which they set their sights, that Brazilian positivists were simultaneously less orthodox and more emphatic in the use of the collective imagination. They were so convinced of their political mission that it would not be unreasonable to call them middle-class bolsheviks. The term also does justice to Comte's admiration of the Jacobins, whom he likely regarded as precursors of the positivist priesthood.

Miguel Lemos and Teixeira Mendes, the two acknowledged Brazilian leaders of orthodox positivism, effected the reorientation of the movement in Brazil. Before their participation, the dominant group was that closest to Émile Littré, a disciple of Comte who rejected the master's post-Clotilde phase. This was the orientation of Pereira Barreto and of the Positivist Society of Rio de Janeiro. It

36. Temple of Humanity,
Rio de Janeiro.

was also the orientation of both Lemos and Teixeira Mendes before
their conversion in Paris, following their contact with Pierre Laffitte,
the leader of the orthodox group in France. On returning to Brazil
in 1881, Lemos immediately sought to take over the leadership of
the Positivist Society in Rio de Janeiro, convincing Laffitte to en-
dorse him for the position. His attitude reflected more than a mere
dispute over power; it was a matter of principle. Lemos could not
accept the fact that the former leader, J. R. de Mendonça, was simultaneously a positivist and a slaveowner. Nor could he accept that
another candidate to the leadership, Álvaro de Oliveira, occupied
the post of professor at the Polytechnic School, thus contradicting
Comte's precepts.[7]

Two years later, in 1883, Lemos broke with Laffitte, who was accused by the Brazilians of being unfaithful to Comte's teachings, especially to those pertaining to positivist occupation of public office.

37. Altar of the Temple of Humanity,
Rio de Janeiro.

In Laffitte's view, the prohibition applied only to the priesthood; it was merely an advisory for other positivists—that is, for the practical ones. Lemos, citing Comte's *Appel aux conservateurs,* argued that the prohibition applied to all positivists, whether theoretical or practical. Various French positivists, such as Jean-François Robinet and Alfred Dubuisson—the latter a personal friend of Lemos—took Laffitte's side. The position of the Brazilian orthodox positivists struck them as a demonstration of Puritanism, of exaggerated faith. From London, Frederic Harrison accused the Brazilians of a childish pietism.

To all appearances, this really was a case of an excessive rigor and an exaggerated preoccupation with following Comte's recommendations to the letter. However, a reading of Lemos's correspondence with Laffitte, which is housed in the Maison d'Auguste Comte in Paris, allows for another interpretation.[8] The letters clearly reveal the political justification of Lemos's actions to other positivists. Lemos interpreted Brazilian reality in a totally nonorthodox way, and one result of that interpretation was a great emphasis on the urgency of political action. Because this is a central point, I quote at some length a passage from one of his letters, dated August 22, 1881:

Here [in Brazil], the liberal and educated classes are those that will bring about the transformation. Strictly speaking, we have no proletariat; our industry is exclusively agrarian; and the rural worker is the Negro slave. This greatly modifies the situation of Brazilian positivists and makes it a more difficult one than that in Paris and London. There, your actions are still latent; you are still like someone lost in the midst of those great cities, where you seek support among the proletariat's elite. Here, on the contrary, we stand out, belonging ourselves to the liberal classes, upon which we act directly; all eyes are on us; our every acts and words immediately become the events of the day. Here, scientific and official circles, far from being like your citadels of reaction, are actually the most modifiable elements, and we obtain from them adherents and sympathizers regularly. All of this demands of Positivism extraordinary activity, so that it may be prepared to attend to the public's needs. Tomorrow we shall have wise men, statesmen, and highly-placed individuals accepting some of our conceptions, or even fully converting to Positivism. We must prove ourselves equal to the task. Considering the circumstances indicated above, however, we shall need not only devotion and activity, but also sufficiently developed organization and discipline.

This is primarily a nonorthodox analysis. Comte never recognized an element of transformation in the liberal classes. Aside from the priesthood itself, he expected regenerative action from certain groups or classes, such as the proletarians, the patricians, and women. The emphasis he placed on each of these groups varied based on its receptiveness. In the period preceding the revolution of 1848, Comte's contact with some workers who were attending his astronomy course led him to view them as the principal messengers of positivism. One of those workers, Magnin, was described by Comte as a model statesman and was selected by him as a member of the triumvirate that would govern France in the final phase. According to Comte, the events of 1848 demonstrated that the proletarians still remained the captives of a revolutionary utopia. He then turned to the patricians, for whom he wrote the *Appel aux conservateurs* (1885). Finally, it seemed to him that the most receptive public would be Catholic women, and for them he wrote the *Catéchisme positiviste.*[9] The liberal classes (middle classes) had no place in the future society, and in France at the time, they seemed overly attracted to either liberalism or to the revolutionary left, two examples of metaphysics that Comte abhorred.

Lemos perceived that the rural proletariat in Brazil did not exist politically and that the urban proletariat was only beginning to form. He also perceived that conservatives were socially the captives of slavery and politically the captives of the principles of liberalism and representative monarchy. Women constituted an accessible element, but they required long-term effort, given the strength of Catholic and patriarchal traditions. Finally, in the middle class, Lemos saw elements capable of being transformed into forces for progress. Liberal professionals with scientific training—engineers, doctors, mathematicians, and most teachers—stood out within this class. Schools of medicine, of engineering, and even of law were the major nuclei of intellectual and political debate and of resistance to slavery.

The social position of the Brazilian orthodox positivists lent itself to such an interpretation. Lemos was the son of a retired naval officer who was unable to pay for his son's education. Teixeira Mendes, his alter ego, was the son of an engineer. The occupational data of the twenty-four individuals who signed a circular letter of December 3, 1883, in which Lemos formalized his break with Laffitte, reinforces this thesis (see table 1).

Table 1.   Signers of the Collective Circular, 1883

Occupation	No.
Student of medicine, engineering, or mathematics	6
Engineer, doctor, or mathematician	7
Civil servant	7
Lawyer, judge	2
Worker, surveyor	2
Total	24

Source: Circulaire collective adressée a tous les vrais disciples d'Auguste Comte, Rio de Janeiro, Au Siège de la Société Positiviste, 1884.

Lemos is excluded from this calculation because, at that time, he was completely dedicated to the positivist priesthood. After the break with Laffitte, he found employment at the National Library. The occupational data reveals that these signers were special individuals. First, all of them had urban occupations; none were peasants or rural landowners. Furthermore, they belonged to the middle class; none was an urban property owner, banker, or merchant. Finally, none of them was part of the political elite. The civil servants among the signers were lycée teachers, or they occupied secondary positions in the administration. Only two represented the traditional, imperial political elite—namely, a lawyer and a judge. The lawyer, however, did not exercise his profession but instead earned his living as a teacher of Portuguese at a lycée. It can be deduced, therefore, that the orthodox positivists not only were of middle-class standing but also represented a specific sector of that stratum—the technical and scientific sector, made up of doctors, engineers, and mathematicians. The civil servants themselves were nearly all former medical school and polytechnic school students. The political elite of the Brazilian empire, in contrast, was dominated by lawyers and judges and, to a lesser degree, rural landowners.

There is an irony, if not a contradiction, in this. The political base on which Lemos judged he could count had more affinity to Littré's way of thinking than to Comteanism; in other words, it was closer to the *Cours de philosophie* than to the *Système de politique positive*. It was a counter-elite that based its power on technical knowledge, on scientism. Lemos sought to mobilize it by employing the instruments of the second, or later, Comte, including religious practices; he found these instruments more suitable for forming a homogeneous and disciplined nucleus of activists. The contradiction generated shockwaves. Several members of the Positivist Society resigned because they could not accept the new orientation. Among them were important republican leaders such as Benjamin Constant and Silva Jardim.

The conflicts were not limited to the religious aspect. They also pertained to the difficulties in convincing the technicians not to accept the state's largesse. Comte's position on this point was clear. In *Appel aux conservateurs,* he stated that during the phase of transition to normal society, both theoretical and practical positivists should limit themselves to advisory influence "even if offered positions of leadership."[10] Here, Lemos stood on solid ground. In a country in which government visibility was great, the quest for public employment was intense, and political ascent was determined by cronyism; to decline positions of power was virtually an act of civic heroism and a rejection of a universal, though much criticized, practice. The resulting moral authority was considerable. The orthodox positivists were perhaps right to believe that, in Brazil, their moral aspects— that is, that their deeds matched their words, marking an absence of hypocrisy—weighed heavily in propaganda. Furthermore, Lemos held that accepting public positions could compromise positivists by exposing them to the flattery and seductions of power and consequently divert them from their supreme objective: to incorporate the proletariat into civilization.[11]

The difficulties pushed the orthodox positivists to redouble their efforts in attracting middle-class groups and the respect of the general public. Undoubtedly, their emphasis on religion had to do with Brazil's strong Catholic tradition and with Comte's belief that Catholics were the most receptive listeners. The orthodox positivists were always careful not to attack Catholicism and not to create incompatibilities, even though Catholics did not extend to them the same courtesy. If the strategy of rapid transformation through the middle class failed, the female public would become an important element. Ample efforts were also underway to attract the urban proletariat.

Orthodox positivists in Brazil seemed more like a political group, one with very specific ideas about its task and how to realize it, than a band of religious fanatics and madmen. To employ a slightly forced comparison, one might even say that they proposed a middle-class bolshevism—that is, a political voluntarism that believed it could accelerate history through the action of a well-organized, homogenous, and disciplined political vanguard, or, in Comte's terminology, through the action of a strongly organized nucleus. As with Leninist bolshevism, this belief did not contradict their underlying philosophy of history. To both the Marxist and the positivist, history is governed by laws and cannot be amended by people. This, however, does not impede its progress. For both philosophies, the belief in laws was actually the source that provided militants with much-needed strength and certainty.

Manipulators of Symbols

By uniting Comtean doctrine with the orthodox strategic vision, the positivists became the principal manipulators of symbols in the Brazilian republic. If doctrine gave them the content of the symbolism, the strategic vision impelled them to action with a greater urgency than that felt by French positivists or European positivists in general, and even by those of a Comtean conviction. For the Brazilian positivists, Brazil stood at the portal of a great transformation, perhaps ready for an evolutionary leap forward. They saw themselves in a privileged position, capable of accelerating the march of history, and so they plunged into political indoctrination with apostolic conviction and energy.

Actions founded on persuasion necessitated the use of symbols. Beyond any doubt, the chief symbols employed were the written and spoken word. It was abundantly used in books, newspapers, publications of the Positivist Church, and public lectures. It was their principal weapon in persuading the middle-class sectors. But the positivists also employed the symbolism of images and rituals, aiming especially at two strategic publics—women and the proletariat—that were less attuned to the written word, at least in Brazil. Reaching these two publics and convincing them of the integrity of positivist doctrine were indispensable conditions for the ultimate success of their assumed task. The fight over images became especially important.

The presence of a positivist such as Benjamin Constant among the founders of the republic was a stroke of luck, but it would have been to no avail if positivist propaganda had not made easier the task of persuasion. The orthodox positivists worked indefatigably to capture the hearts and minds of the citizenry through the battle of symbols as well as their struggles over monuments, over the myth of Tiradentes, over the republican flag, and over the feminine allegory. Their actions recalled those of other modern revolutionaries, from David to the socialist realists.

The same social conditions that led orthodox positivists to believe that the role of political protagonist would fall to the educated classes led them to influence the elites, primarily. However, in the cases where popular traditions backed their political acts, they deserve credit for substantially contributing to the construction of the few remnants of the republican collective imagination.

CONCLUSION

Republican movements in Brazil failed in their efforts to expand the legitimacy of the new regime beyond the confining borders delineated by the victors. They were incapable of creating a popular republican imagery. In certain respects, they attained some degree of success. However, these small gains resulted from compromises with imperial tradition or religious values. Their efforts were insufficient to overcome the barrier formed by the lack of popular involvement in the founding of the new regime. Lacking roots in collective experience, republican symbolism fell by the wayside, as especially exemplified in the case of feminine allegory.

Even today, the liveliest debate inevitably centers on the myth of origin and republican utopias. It is an ideological and historical debate restricted to a small circle of the regime's beneficiaries. Even in this circle, the inconclusive nature of the Brazilian republic is evident: throughout its more than one hundred years of existence, it has been unable to establish a minimal consensus among its followers. The alternatives offered in the early days still appear desirable and feasible to many. When the liberal-democratic model gains strength, there are still powerful pockets of Jacobinism and positivist vestiges that cling tenaciously to the flanks of the republic. Nor is there any certainty that the modern vision of Deodorism is defunct, once and for all.

The lack of a republican identity and the persistent emergence of conflicting views also help us understand the success of the figure of the hero, as personified by Tiradentes. The republican hero par excellence is multifaceted, ambiguous, and divided. Various factions vie for him: he serves the right, the center, and the left. He is Christ and civic hero; he is martyr and liberator; he is civilian and soldier; he is both the symbol of the *patria* and symbol of the subversive. The iconography reflects these vacillations. Bearded or beardless, in tunic or uniform, as prisoner or second lieutenant, contrite or rebellious: such is the battle for his image, for the image of the republic.

He remains the republican hero by managing to absorb all these divisions without losing his identity. Despite the challenges that emerge from new religious movements, the image of the Virgin of Aparecida is perhaps still that which most successfully grants a sense of national community to vast sectors of the populace; a sense that, in the absence of a republican civic-mindedness, could only come from outside the political domain. The quartered Tiradentes in the arms of the Virgin of Aparecida: this would be the perfect Brazilian, civic-religious *pietà*. The nation exhibits the body of its people in pieces, a body that the republic is still unable to reconstitute.

NOTES

Introduction

1. See José Murilo de Carvalho, *Os bestializados: O Rio de Janeiro e a República que não foi.*

2. On social imagery, see Bronislaw Baczko, *Les imaginaires sociaux: Mémoires et espoirs collectifs.*

3. On the importance of political myths, see Raoul Girardet, *Mitos e mitologias políticas.*

4. Cited in Baczko, *Les imaginaires sociaux,* 54.

5. On David, see Marie-Catherine Sahut and Régis Michel, *David: L'art et la politique.*

6. The report is reproduced in Joshua C. Taylor, ed., *Nineteenth-Century Theories of Art,* 44–45.

7. See the testimony given to *O Paiz,* November 20, 1912.

8. The salutation "Health and Brotherhood" provoked a semantic controversy at the time. Many critics of orthodox positivism argued that it was a mistranslation of the French *Salut et Fraternité.* The correct phrase, according to them, was "Greetings and Brotherhood." For the positivists' response justifying their translation, see R. Teixeira Mendes, *A bandeira nacional,* 18–19.

9. Baczko, *Les imaginaires sociaux,* 54.

10. On Lincoln's twofold image, see David Donald, "The Folklore Lincoln," in Corda and Gerster, eds., *Myth and the American Experience,* 2:43–54.

11. For more on the subject, see E. S. Whittlesey, *Symbols and Legends in Western Art: A Museum Guide.*

chapter one. Republican Utopias

A modified version of this chapter was published as "Entre a liberdade dos antigos e a dos modernos: A República no Brasil," *Dados: Revista de Ciências Sociais* 32, no. 3 (1989): 265–80.

1. See Benjamin Constant, *De la liberté chez les modernes,* ed. Gauchet, 491–515.

2. For the examination of the thinking of the founders of the American republic, I have made use of Gerald Stourzh's *Alexander Hamilton and the Idea of Republican Government.*

3. The concept of *pouvoir royal* was developed in Constant's *Principles de politique,* published in 1819 and included in *De la liberté chez les modernes,* cited above.

4. For the discussion of the idea of the republic in France, I have used the excellent work by Claude Nicolet, *L'idée républicaine en France (1789–1924).* Chapter 4 of this work discusses the relationships between positivism and the Third Republic.

5 Until now, the best discussion of the concept of representation, which I have used here, is that of Hanna Fenichel Pitkin, *The Concept of Representation.*

6. See Barrington Moore, Jr., *Social Origins of Dictatorship and Democracy: Lord and Peasant in the Making of the Modern World.*

7. The influence of French administrative law is evident in the principal book written about political organization during the empire: *Ensaio sobre o direito administrativo,* by Viscount Uruguai. The contradictions of the French policy allowed for the French influence on both radicals and conservatives. Viscount Uruguai was the main theorist for monarchical conservatism.

8. On positivism in Rio Grande do Sul, see Paulo Carneiro, ed., *Idéias políticas de Júlio de Castilhos.*

9. See the discussion of this theme in J. G. A. Pocock, "Civic Humanism and Its Role in Anglo-American Thought," in his *Politics, Language, and Time,* 80–103.

10. I reproduce here part of the discussion in my *Os bestializados: O Rio de Janeiro e a República que não foi,* 140–60. See Edmond Demolins, *A quoi tient la supériorité des Anglo-Saxons;* Alberto Sales, "Balanço político—necessidade de uma reforma constitucional," *O Estado de São Paulo,* July 18, 1901; and Sílvio Romero, *O Brasil social.*

11. Aníbal Falcão, *Fórmula da civilização brasileira.*

12. Richard M. Morse, *O espelho de Próspero: Cultura e idéias nas Américas.*

13. See Alberto Torres, *A organização nacional,* 297.

chapter two.   The Proclamations of the Republic

A summary version of this chapter was published in *Ciência Hoje* 59 (November 1989): 26–33.

1. See Tobias Monteiro, *Pesquisas e depoimentos para a história,* 6.

2. Blondel to Spuller, Rio de Janeiro, January 4, 1890. Quai d'Orsay, *Correspondance politique, Brésil, 1871–1896.*

3. Obviously, the Benjamin Constant in this chapter is the Brazilian military figure and not the French theorist discussed in chapter 1.

4. The Fonsecas formed a veritable clan within the army. Deodoro had no sons, but he had an abundance of brothers and nephews. Among the relatives who played some role in the republican conspiracy were his brothers Pedro Paulino, an honorary colonel; João Severiano, a medical general; and Marshal Hermes Ernesto, a commander of arms in Bahia who opposed the movement. The most active relatives were the nephews, among whom were Captain Hermes, the son-in-law of Pedro Paulino and future president of Brazil; Captains Percílio, Mário Hermes, and Pedro Paulo; and Lieutenant Clodoaldo. Captain Pedro Paulo was inside the General Headquarters on November 15 and, according to some versions, opened the gates for his uncle's entrance.

5. See Ernesto Senna, *Deodoro: Subsídios para a história,* 119. Out of the meetings came the pamphlet *Quinze de novembro: Contestação a Suetônio* (1898). The author of one account of November 15 that was considered favorable to Quintino Bocaiúva used the pseudonym "Suetônio."

6. See the lengthy testimony by Sebastião Bandeira in Ernesto Senna, *Deodoro.* The quotation is from p. 90.

7. The Military Question refers to a series of conflicts between army officers and the government that took place between 1886 and 1889. The proclamation of the Brazilian republic can be regarded as its final episode.

8. See Ernesto Senna, *Deodoro,* 20.

9. See R. Magalhães Júnior, *Deodoro: A espada contra o império,* 2:48–49. See also the statement of then general Hermes to the *Jornal do Commercio,* November 15, 1903.

10. See the statement by Serzedelo Correia to the *Jornal do Commercio,* November 26, 1903. The importance of the emperor's illness to the fall of the monarchy, after the Military Question, is emphasized by Wanderley Pinho in "A Questão Militar e a República," *Revista do Brasil* 2, no. 17 (November 1939): 23–30.

11. See the statement by Major Roberto Trompowsky to the *Jornal do Commercio,* November 26, 1889. Trompowsky was Saraiva's messenger.

12. See Magalhães Júnior, *Deodoro,* 2:49.

13. See R. Teixeira Mendes, *Benjamin Constant: Esboço de uma apreciação sintética da vida e da obra do fundador da República brasileira.* Another illustrious representative of the Benjamin Constant group is Vicente Licínio Cardoso. Consult his chapter on Constant in his collection *À margem da história da República,* 2d ed., 2:81–94.

14. According to statements by Medeiros e Albuquerque in *Quando eu era vivo,* 104–5.

15. The Positivist Church and Apostolate of Brazil were founded by Miguel Lemos and Teixeira Mendes with the purpose of introducing to their country the practice of orthodox positivism, as represented in France at that time by Pierre Laffitte. For more on the positivists, see chapter 6.

16. On Jacobinism, see Suely Robles Reis de Queiroz, *Os radicais da República: Jacobinismo: ideologia e ação, 1893–1897.*

17. See R. Teixeira Mendes, *Benjamin Constant,* 536–38. A similar conception to that of the monument was the plan for an oil painting by Eduardo de Sá, dealing with the proclamation of the republic. In the painting, Constant appears as a central figure and final link in the chain that begins with Tiradentes and passes through José Bonifácio. The republic also appears joined to humanity. The painting apparently was never completed. See *O Paiz,* November 15, 1899.

18. "Caramuru" (1781), a poem by Santa Rita Durão; "A Cachoeira de Paulo Afonso" (1876), by Castro Alves; "Y Juca-Pirama" (1857), by Gonçalves Dias; and "Anchieta ou o Evangelho nas Selvas" (1875), by Fagundes Varela.

19. On the monument to Floriano Peixoto, see A. R. Gomes de Castro, *O monumento a Floriano por Eduardo de Sá.* Major Gomes de Castro, a positivist and Florianista, was chairman of the commission to construct the monument. The comment by Francisco de Assis Barbosa is from the preface ("Para uma reavalição de Floriano") that he wrote for the second edition of Sérgio Correia da Costa, *A diplomacia do marechal,* xix.

20. For examples of criticisms of the monument, see *O Paiz,* May 10, 1904. The editorial in Quintino Bocaiúva's newspaper censures the commission for imposing limitations on the competing sculptors who submitted plans for the monument. The result was that plans were poorly done; they lacked originality, were ridiculously complicated, and censurably partisan. According to the editorialist, to erect such a monument would be "to give the cultured world a melancholy testament to fanaticism and to bring upon ourselves a most unhappy ridicule." But after a six-year battle, the monument was erected as the commission and the major desired.

21. See *O monumento a Júlio de Castilhos,* a leaflet published by the state of Rio Grande do Sul, in which Eduardo de Sá expounds the aesthetic theo-

ries of positivism and describes the concept of the work. See also Gomes de Castro, *O monumento a Floriano,* 9–35.

22. See Eduardo Silva, ed., *Idéias políticas de Quintino Bocaiúva,* 1:643.

23. See Coleção Saldanha Marinho, Arquivo Geral da Cidade do Rio de Janeiro, 41-1-59, vol. 12, pp. 122–25.

24. Ibid., 41-1-61, vol. 14, p. 45, letter from Saldanha Marinho to Francisco Glicério dated October 3, 1888.

25. See above note.

26. See the interview of Aristides Lobo in Tobias Monteiro, *Pesquisas e depoimentos,* 199–213. See also Eduardo Silva, *Idéias políticas de Quintino Bocaiúva,* 1:645.

27. See Tobias Monteiro, *Pesquisas e depoimentos,* 211. See also Leôncio Correia, *A verdade histórica sobre o 15 de novembro,* 85, 256, 262. Captain Mário Hermes's phrase is in *Deodoro e a verdade histórica,* 151–53. Perhaps because of this hesitation, the victors proclaimed the republican regime *provisionally,* waiting for a popular consultation to decide on the definitive form of government.

28. See M. E. de Campos Porto, *Apontamentos para a história da República dos Estados Unidos do Brasil,* xiii.

29. See the statement of Arthur Azevedo in *O Paiz,* November 17, 1902.

30. Ibid.

31. *Anais da Assembléia Constituinte,* 1891, 2:637–50, and 3:293–94.

32. The episode is recounted in Ernesto Senna, *Deodoro,* 106.

33. Regarding the military in 1930s, see José Murilo de Carvalho, "Forças armadas e política, 1930–1945," in *A revolução de 30: Seminário internacional,* 109–50. I am grateful to Professor Mário Barata for information on the transfer of the statue of Benjamin Constant.

34. The potential for generating controversy was clear at the National Conference on the History of Propaganda, Proclamation and Consolidation of the Republic in Brazil, organized by the Historical and Geographical Institute (IHGB) in November 1989. The positions and arguments from a hundred years earlier were repeated, sometimes almost literally. The conference's proceedings were published in *Anais do Congresso Nacional de História da Propaganda, Proclamação e Consolidação da República no Brasil.*

chapter three.   Tiradentes

1. See Eduardo Prado, *Fastos da ditadura militar no Brasil,* 287. Medeiros e Albuquerque confirms the unmilitary personality of Benjamin Constant. He was "extremely gentle," pleasant, and soft-spoken. Introspective and

absentminded, he often had "the appearance of a sleepwalker." See Medeiros e Albuquerque, *Quando eu era vivo,* 109–13.

2. The survival of Florianism in the popular imagination of Rio Janeiro was detected and analyzed by Maria Helena Cabral de Almeida Cardoso in "A herança arcaica do jacobinismo," presented at the National Conference on the History of the Propaganda, Proclamation, and Consolidation of the Republic in Brazil, IHGB, Rio de Janeiro, November 1989.

3. The comical appears in Mendes Fradique's *História do Brasil pelo método confuso.* In an imaginary trial of Pedro II, the character Brazil is asleep the entire time. At the end, she wakes up and, still half dazed, asks, referring to a lottery based on the names of animals, "What animal won?" "Deodoro," they tell her (168).

4. Even today, in a country that frequently deprecates and ridicules heroes, Tiradentes remains respectfully recognized as a national hero. Paulo Miceli notes the plausibility of this hypothesis in his *O mito do herói nacional,* 22–25. According to Miceli, Tiradentes is the favorite hero among first- and second-grade pupils.

5. The information can be found in Hélio Moro Mariante, "Revolução de 1893," presented at the National Conference on the History of the Propaganda, Proclamation, and Consolidation of the Republic in Brazil, IHGB, Rio de Janeiro, November 1989.

6. A *capitania* was an administrative division of the Portuguese colony in America.

7. See "Memória do êxito que teve a conjuração de Minas e dos factos relativos a ella acontecidos nesta cidade do Rio de Janeiro desde o dia 17 até 26 de abril de 1792," *Revista do IHGB* 62–63, t. 44 (1881): 140–60. Hangings in Rio de Janeiro were generally occasions for great excitement and pleasure among the people. The sadness caused by the death of Tiradentes was an exception. On hangings, see Mello Moraes Filho, *Festas e tradições populares do Brasil,* 218–24.

8. See "Últimos momentos dos Inconfidentes de 1789 pelo frade que os assistiu de confissão," *Revista do IHGB* 62–63, t. 44 (1881): 161–86.

9. The complaints are by Joaquim Silvério dos Reis in a letter to Martinho de Melo e Castro, according to information from Augusto de Lima Júnior in his *Notícias históricas,* as cited by Waldemar de Almeida Barbosa in *A verdade sobre Tiradentes,* 59. Another informer, the Portuguese colonel Basílio de Brito, admitted in a testamentary letter that "all the people in Minas and even in Brazil felt implacable hatred for me" and that he feared assassination. See Eduardo Machado de Castro, "A Inconfidência Mineira: Narrativa popular," *Revista do Arquivo Público Mineiro* 6, fasc. 1 (January–March 1901): 1145.

10. See the document found in the Public Library of Évora, reproduced in part by Waldemar de Almeida Barbosa in *A verdade sobre Tiradentes,* 35–36. According to the document, a letter, some families left Vila Rica, "large mining concerns were lost," and the most learned and needed men became dead to society. An eyewitness to the departure of the "prisoners of the queen" from Vila Rica to Rio de Janeiro also records the fact that "a general sadness enveloped the town," streets were deserted, houses shut. See Eduardo Machado de Castro, "A Inconfidência Mineira," 1113.

11. Richard Burton, *Viagem a Rio de Janeiro e Morro Velho.*

12. The Brazilian empire was divided into the First Reign (1822–31), the Regency (1831–40), and the Second Reign (1840–89).

13. José Antônio Marinho, *História da Revolução de 1842,* 42. The letter from the priest Manuel Rodrigues da Costa is transcribed on pp. 71–73 of that book, first published in 1844.

14. Robert Southey, *História do Brasil,* vol. 6, chap. 43. See also *Revista do IHGB* 8 (1846): 297–310.

15. Charles Ribeyrolles, *Brasil pitoresco,* 47–95.

16. Antônio Frederico de Castro Alves, "Gonzaga ou a revolução de Minas," in *Obras completas,* 579–661. The first edition of the play is from 1875. Castro Alves's rebels were already speaking of the French Revolution, which had not happened at the time, and singing the *Marseillaise,* which would not be composed until 1792.

17. Pedro Luís Pereira de Sousa, "O Tiradentes," in *Tiradentes: Homenagem ao primeiro mártir da liberdade,* April 21, 1888.

18. On the incidents of 1893, see *O Paiz* for April 19, 20, and 21 of that year; and the *Jornal do Brasil* and *Jornal do Commercio* for April 20. On the Palácio Tiradentes, see *Livro do centenário da Câmara dos Deputados (1826–1926).* The monument built in Ouro Preto dates from 1892. The documents from the Tiradentes Club, now in the National Historical Museum, also provide rich material on the struggle over the memory of the hero.

19. See J. Norberto de Sousa Silva, *História da Conjuração Mineira.* Sousa Silva's explanations of the reasons behind hastening the work's publication and having opposed the monument's construction can be found in his article "O Tiradentes perante os historiadores oculares de seu tempo," *Revista do IHGB* 62–63, t. 44 (1888): 131–39. The citation is on p. 138. Sousa Silva mocks the commemorations of Tiradentes's martyrdom by claiming that they would have pleased Count Rezende. This is like mocking Christian celebrations of Christ's passion by claiming they would please Annas and Caiphas.

20. The first reactions appeared in the republican press. Sousa Silva mentions, without providing complete references, several articles in *A República* and *A Reforma,* the latter signed by "A Mineiro." He also mentions an

article by Aristides Maia in *A República,* the organ of the Academic Republican Club of São Paulo. The aforementioned criticism by Eduardo Machado de Castro, written in 1896, was published in 1901. The battle resumed in 1922 with Lúcio José dos Santos, in a work presented to the Conference on National History, sponsored by the Historical Institute. Around that same time, Assis Cintra took up Sousa Silva's positions again. More recently, the book by Waldemar de Almeida Barbosa, already mentioned, again virulently attacked Sousa Silva. The preface by Lúcio José dos Santos states openly that the author's objective is to put an end to the deceptions of Sousa Silva, who attempted "to denigrate or efface the exceptional figure of Lt. Joaquim José." The author uses an even stronger expression: Sousa Silva sought "to ridicule the figure of Tiradentes." See Barbosa, *A verdade sobre Tiradentes,* 7, 17. Also consult chap. 13 of that work for an examination of Sousa Silva's influence on later authors, including Capistrano de Abreu, João Ribeiro, and Pedro Calmon. Augusto de Lima Júnior and Waldemar de Almeida Barbosa also defended the representation of Tiradentes as a beardless lieutenant, in contrast with the mystic figure presented by Sousa Silva. In recent times the anti-Tiradentes view has been represented by Sérgio Faraco. See his *Tiradentes: A alguma verdade (ainda que tardia).*

21. Sousa Silva, "O Tiradentes perante os historiadores," 132.

22. Cited in "Advertência," in Sousa Silva, *História da Conjuração Mineira,* vii. In defense of this statement, it could be claimed that it was the means found by courtiers to justify the treatment of such a delicate matter before Pedro II.

23. Sousa Silva, "O Tiradentes perante os historiadores," 151.

24. The reactions were recorded by Sousa Silva in "O Tiradentes perante os historiadores." Many of them doubtless were due to the fact that Sousa Silva's opponents did not have access to the documents he used. But what is important here is the republican admission, as seconded by Sousa Silva, that the mystic diminished, if not nullified, the patriot.

25. See João Pinheiro, Antônio Olinto, and Nicésio Machado, "Minas Gerais," *O Tiradentes* 7 (1888).

26. *O Paiz,* April 21, 1890.

27. Herculano Gomes Mathias asked twenty schoolchildren to identify the figure represented in Décio Villares's drawing. Three said it was Christ; five saw Tiradentes in it; one, Felipe dos Santos; one, Antônio Conselheiro. See Mathias, *Tiradentes através da imagem,* 29.

28. See "Tiradentes," *O Paiz,* April 21, 1896.

29. The commemoration of Tiradentes in 1902 took on a special brilliance. According to *O Paiz,* three thousand people signed a document on April 18 by which the city government took possession of the land on which the monument to Tiradentes was to be built. On this occasion, Eduardo de

Sá's painting *The Reading of the Sentence* was also unveiled. At the celebration on April 21, the overture to *O Guarani* and a hymn to Tiradentes, with music by the maestro Francisco Flores and lyrics by Luís Delfino, were performed. The editorial in *O Paiz* for April 19 refers to Tiradentes as a hero and martyr who, in republican worship, is a demigod. But on the same occasion (*O Paiz*, April 21), an article by Féliz Bocaiúva entitled "Os olvidados" notes the changes in the nature of the solemnities. According to Bocaiúva, *arrivistes* were taking over the celebrations. The republicans of propaganda and of the heroic times, those who raised the ideal of Tiradentes and who were his legitimate successors, were being marginalized and were being forgotten in the "civic liturgies of patriotism." Perhaps this was because those were times in which, according to the author, the republic dragged the unpolluted, white wing of its ideals through the mud.

30. José Pereira de Araújo, *Tiradentes,* unbound publication of the Positivist Center, 1884.

31. See Visconde de Taunay, "O Tiradentes e nós, monarquistas," in his *Império e República,* 5–15.

32. Ubaldino do Amaral, "Tiradentes," address at the commemoration of the hundred and second anniversary of the torture of Tiradentes, on April 21, 1894, in the hall of the Ginásio Nacional.

33. See Viriato Correia, *Tiradentes: Comédia histórica em três atos e sete quadros.*

34. Curiously, the military government refused to adopt the representation proposed by Walsht Rodrigues, despite pressure from critics of Sousa Silva, such as Augusto de Lima Júnior. The 1966 decree, complementing the 1965 law, ordered the use of the sculpture by Francisco Andrade as the model in representations of Tiradentes. The statue is a compromise between the civic and religious versions. Tiradentes appears there in the white garb of the condemned, on his way to the hanging, but at the same time maintains a defiant and rebellious attitude.

35. See Augusto Boal and Gianfrancesco Guarnieri, *Arena canta Tiradentes.* It is worth noting that the Inconfidência in general and Tiradentes in particular are themes that have most inspired Brazilian artists, a powerful indication of the attraction they have exercised over the national imagination. These artists include novelists, poets, playwrights, musicians, plastic artists, and film directors. In the nineteenth century, their numbers include Bernardo Guimarães, Castro Alves, Pedro Luís, Pedro Américo, Décio Villares, and Antônio Parreiras, and more recently, Portinari, Glauco Rodrigues, Cecília Meirelles, Gilberto de Alencar, Autran Dourado, and Joaquim Pedro de Andrade. Erudite art allies itself to popular art, from the *cordel* to the *samba-enredo.* Who cannot recall the Império Serrano samba school singing Mano Décio da Viola's lyrics: "Joaquim José da Silva Xavier / Died on April 21 / for

the independence of Brazil / He was betrayed but never betrayed / the Inconfidência of Minas Gerais"?

chapter four.   The Republic as a Woman

1. Here, I closely follow the excellent work of Maurice Agulhon, *Marianne au combat: L'imagerie et la symbolique républicaines de 1789 a 1880.* The quotation is on p. 2. See also, by the same author, "Esquisse pour une archéologie de la République: L'allégorie civique féminine," *Annales ESC* 28 (1973): 5–34.

2. About the contest of 1848, as well as about Delacroix and Daumier, see T. J. Clark, *The Absolute Bourgeois: Artists and Politics in France, 1848–1851.*

3. Agulhon, *Marianne au combat,* 164.

4. The transition from nude woman to bare-chested man in the symbolism of the popular movement is discussed by Eric J. Hobsbawm in "Homem e mulher: Imagens da esquerda," a chapter in his *Mundos do Trabalho: Novas estudios sobre história operária* (English edition, *Worlds of Labour: Further Studies in the History of Labour*), 123–47.

5. Third reign refers to a third ruler, Isabel, after her grandfather and father.

6. See Hippolyto da Silva, *Humorismo da propaganda republicana,* 2. "To kill? Yes!" shouted Silva Jardim, referring to Count d'Eu in a speech of February 1888. See Antônio da Silva Jardim, *Propaganda republicana* (1888–1889), 85.

7. See Álvaro Cotrim (Alvarus), "O 15 de novembro na imprensa ilustrada," *Jornal do Brasil,* November 15, 1973. See also the excellent *História da caricatura no Brasil* by Herman Lima.

8. I thank Claudio Veiga, president of the Bahian Academy of Letters, for access to the photo and information about the painting and the painter.

9. The Comtean view of woman, faithfully incorporated by orthodox positivists in Brazil, can be found in R. Teixeira Mendes, *A mulher: Sua preeminência social e moral segundo os ensinos da verdadeira ciência positiva.* This is a speech given by Teixeira Mendes on November 27, 1908.

10. Eduardo de Sá himself expounded the positivist aesthetic ideas in the pamphlet *O monumento a Júlio de Castilhos.*

11. See also the feminine figures on the principal altar of the Chapel of Humanity in Rio de Janeiro and in Clotilde's home in Paris. The former is by Décio Villares, the latter by Eduardo de Sá. Both clearly reproduce the facial features of Clotilde.

12. On art politics and the first artistic exhibitions after the proclamation of the republic, see Donato Mello Júnior, "As primeiras exposições de

belas-artes na República," a work presented at the National Conference on the History of Propaganda, Proclamation and Consolidation of the Republic in Brazil, IHGB, November 1989. On the constitution, see the paintings of Aurélio de Figueiredo, *O compromisso constitucional,* and E. Visconti, *A Constituição de 1891.*

13. I thank Francisco de Assis Barbosa for having called my attention to this episode. Fausto Cardoso's denunciation can be found in *Anais da Câmara dos Deputados,* vols. 5 and 6, 1900, pp. 62, 144, and 145.]In his speech, the orator exhibited the treasury note with the portrait. A reproduction of the bill can be found in the book *Cédulas brasileiras da República: Emissões do Tesouro Nacional,* 19, published by the Bank of Brazil. The note in discussion is number 9, from 1900. According to information in the book, the picture is based on the painting by the Austrian Conrado Kiesel. Entitled *Saudade,* it represents a Brazilian woman he met in Vienna.

14. See Coelho Neto, *Fogo fátuo,* 229–38.

15. See Mendes Fradique, *História do Brasil pelo método confuso,* 153–58. I thank Isabel Lustosa for calling my attention to this reference.

16. On the already semi-mythified use of figures such as Saint-Milhier's heroine and the citizen Bourgougnoux by salon painters of year II, see Claude Langlois, "Les dérives vendéennes de l'imaginaire révolutionnaire," *Annales ESC* 3 (May–June 1988): 771–97. On the role of women in the French Revolution, see *Les femmes et la Révolution, 1789–1794,* by Paule-Marie Duhet.

17. It might be asked why David did not represent the republic in a way that was inspired by some of the heroines of the time. When he used the female figure, he resorted either to living models, as in the *Feast of the Supreme Being,* or to examples from antiquity, as in *The Sabine Women.* The reason could have been his neoclassical aesthetic convictions. But such convictions did not stop him from painting the renowned *Death of Marat.* Perhaps, like other revolutionaries, the concrete actions of women in the French Revolution made him uncomfortable.

18. See Esther de Viveiros, *Rondon conta sua vida,* 53–54, 58.

19. The adolescent Di Cavalcanti recounts his surprise at seeing the portrait of the emperor in a prostitute's bedroom, after the advent of the republic. Cited in Eduardo Silva, *As queixas do povo,* 61–64.

20. See Gilberto Freyre, *Ordem e progresso,* 1:viii, 21–24.

21. On the worship of Our Lady of Aparecida and its political connotations, see Rubem César Fernandes, "Aparecida: nossa rainha, senhora e mãe, saravá!" in Viola Sachs et al., *Brasil e Estados Unidos: religião e identidade nacional.* See also Mário Carelli, "Quelques réflexions autour de l'indéfinition de l'allégorie féminine du Brésil," *Cahiers du Brésil Contemporain,* Paris, Centre de Recherches sur le Brésil Contemporain, 12 (1990): 59–68.

22. For a history of painting in Brazil, see Quirino Campofiorito, *História da pintura brasileira no século XIX.*

23. Maria Cristina Castilho Costa, in her master's thesis, "O retrato feminino na pintura brasileira, 1800–1950," University of São Paulo, 1985, sees a change in the view of the woman in this period. Portraits, which are more realistic in style in the first half of the nineteenth century, acquire romantic traits in the second half, when the characteristics of fragility, gentleness, and submission are emphasized.

24. For an attempted answer, see Mário Carelli, "Quelques réflexions autour de l'indéfinition de l'allégorie féminine du Brésil." A very rare example of the nation represented as an Indian woman is found in *Revista Illustrada,* no. 577, February 8, 1890.

25. On the women of Rio de Janeiro as seen by foreign travelers, see Miriam Lifchitz Moreira Leite, *A mulher no Rio de Janeiro no século XIX.* The idealization of woman by male writers is discussed by Maria Thereza Caiuby Crescenti Bernardes in *Mulheres de ontem? Rio de Janeiro—século XIX.*

26. *O Paiz,* November 13, 1902.

chapter five.   Flag and Anthem

1. About this episode, see Ernesto Senna, *Deodoro: Subsídios para a história,* 53–54.

2. On the tricolor flag of the French, see Raoul Girardet, "Les trois couleurs, ni blanc, ni rouge," in Pierre Nora, ed., *Les lieux de mémoire,* vol. 1, *La République,* 5–35.

3. See the series of statements under the title "Uma dúvida histórica: A bandeira da revolução de 1889." The statement by Captain Souza Barros was published on November 20.

4. See *O Paiz,* April 21, 1894.

5. The statement by Augusto Malta is in *O Paiz,* November 19, 1912.

6. See *O Paiz,* November 17, 1912.

7. On the changing of flags on the *Alagoas,* see Tobias Monteiro, *Pesquisas e depoimentos,* 305. Álvaro Cotrim (Alvarus) also states that the flag hoisted in the Municipal Chamber, reproduced in *O Mequetrefe,* was raised on the *Alagoas,* which, as we have seen, is impossible. See Álvaro Cotrim, "O 15 de novembro na imprensa ilustrada," *Jornal do Brasil,* November 15, 1973. According to Cotrim, it had thirteen horizontal stripes, and the lozenge had a blue background.

8. See, for example, the testimony of Major Dias Jacaré in *O Paiz,* November 16, 1912. Sampaio Ferraz, president of the Tiradentes Club in 1889,

confuses things even further in 1912. He states that on November 15 he delivered a tricolor flag to be raised in the Chamber. See *O Paiz,* November 16, 1912. The black background is confirmed by Emílio Ribeiro in *O Paiz,* November 17, 1912.

9. The positivists' position is well documented in the collection organized by the Positivist Church and the Positivist Apostolate of Brazil under the title *A bandeira nacional,* by R. Teixeira Mendes. In it are found the principal articles by Teixeira Mendes and Miguel Lemos relating to the fact. I use the third edition, from 1958.

10. See Teixeira Mendes, *A bandeira nacional,* 5–10.

11. The concern about adopting the American symbol is explicit in Benjamin Constant's biography by Teixeira Mendes, published in 1891. See his *Benjamin Constant,* 376–77.

12. See *Diário do Commercio,* November 24, 1889. For Teixeira Mendes's reply, see his *A bandeira nacional,* 11–14.

13. The journalist was probably Eduardo Prado, who at the time, writing from Europe, made tremendous attacks against the new regime.

14. See Teixeira Mendes, *A bandeira nacional,* 14–21.

15. See Eduardo Prado, *A bandeira nacional.* The error in the position of the constellations and even in the location of the South Pole in the lower part of the design is confirmed by Ronaldo Rogério de Freitas Mourão in "A bandeira da República," *Revista do Brasil* 4, no. 8 (1989): 84–90. Luiz Cruls, then director of the Astronomical Observatory, supported Pereira Reis in contradicting the opinion of the French Astronomical Society, stating that it was common in geographical atlases to show the north above and the south below.

16. See *Diário de Notícias,* September 8, 1892, and Coelho Neto, *Fogo fátuo,* 233.

17. The two documents are included in Teixeira Mendes, *A bandeira nacional,* 49–55.

18. Valadão's proposal was presented to congress on September 1, 1892. The flag was defended by José Beviláqua, a soldier and positivist, in terms that repeated, nearly verbatim, Teixeira Mendes's arguments. See *Anais da Câmara dos Deputados,* 1892, vol. 5, pp. 92, 352, 381–82, 434. Peixoto's opposition to the positivist flag is confirmed by Serzedelo Correia in *Páginas do passado,* 85–86. Valadão's proposal had important backers, including the press. The *Jornal do Brasil* opined favorably about the change, accusing the provisional government of having adopted an emblem "inspired by a sectarian group, insignificant, and extremely tiny in number; mediocre in social value, unsympathetic and unsupportive to the country; representing not the national sentiment but a new ultramontanism lead by a hidden, decrepit French

philosopher." See the edition of September 8, 1892. In 1905 a new proposal that sought to remove the positivist motto was presented to the Chamber. See Agenor de Roure, "A bandeira nacional," *Kosmos* 4, no. 3 (March 1907).

19. See Alvaro Cotrim, "O 15 de novembro na imprensa ilustrada," *Jornal do Brasil,* November 15, 1973.

20. In his memoirs, Medeiros e Albuquerque mentions the presence of Teixeira Mendes at the first meeting of the provisional government, on the night of November 15. According to his statement, the positivist leader went from person to person, exhorting them, "Proclaim the dictatorship! Proclaim the dictatorship!" See Medeiros e Albuquerque, *Quando eu era vivo,* 104–5.

21. Medeiros e Albuquerque, *Quando eu era vivo,* 90.

22. It was "a very delicate date," as the French representative, Amelot, wrote to Minister Spuller in a letter of July 10, 1889. *Ministère des Affaires Étrangères, Correspondance politique, Brésil,* vol. 53.

23. The information on the history of the *Marseillaise* summarized here comes from Michel Vovelle, "La marseillaise: La guerre ou la paix," in Pierre Nora, ed., *Les lieux de mémoire,* vol. 1, *La République,* 85–136.

24. Vovelle, "La marseillaise," 96.

25. Vovelle, "La marseillaise," 119.

26. Spiritism, originally based on the work of French educator Allan Kardec (1804–69), is a fairly widely practiced religion in Brazil.

27. The text, undated, is found in the National Library, Music Section, Archive of Augusto D. N. D'Almeida, Collection Ayres de Andrade.

28. Medeiros e Albuquerque confirms that the republicans sang the *Marseillaise* upon leaving their meetings. The fact led him to write a Brazilian lyric, which he presented to Silva Jardim and which was adopted. See his *Quando eu era vivo,* 90–91, 116–17.

29. See, for example, the article by Oscar Guanabarino, "O hino nacional," in *O Paiz,* January 17, 1890. See also the news sections of *Jornal do Commercio* and of *O Paiz,* January 16, 1890, and R. Magalhães Júnior, *Deodoro: A espada contra o Império,* 2:133–39. *O Paiz* for January 16, 1890, states that there was no premeditation. The episode came from the "voice of the people that spoke then." Francisco Manuel da Silva's anthem was generally only performed in its instrumental form, hence the reason it was called the *Ta-ra-ta-ta-tchin.* It was composed just after Brazil achieved independence from Portugal in 1822 but was only sung for the first time in 1831, after the abdication, with lyrics by Ovídio Saraiva de Carvalho e Silva. The lyrics were very anti-Portuguese and, little by little, were abandoned. Another set of lyrics by an anonymous author emerged on the occasion of Pedro II's coronation and was adapted to that event. Because of their restricted character, they also had no greater influence. The fact that only the music survived undoubtedly facilitated the acceptance of the old anthem by the new regime. On this subject,

see Max Fleiuss, "Francisco Manuel da Silva e o hino nacional," presented at the IHGB on October 12, 1916.

30. See Raul Pompéia, *Obras,* 250–51, 256–57. See also Oscar Guanabarino, "O hino nacional," cited above.

31. On the extraordinary history of the New Orleans pianist, see Louis Moreau Gottschalk, *Notes of a Pianist.* His adventure in Rio is described in Francisco Curt Lange, *Vida y muerte de Louis Moreau Gottschalk en Río de Janeiro, 1869.*

32. See *O Paiz,* January 21, 1890, unsigned article entitled "O hino da proclamação." See also Oscar Guanabarino, "O hino nacional."

33. See Thomé Júnior, "Já é tempo!" *Revista Illustrada,* no. 590 (May 1890): 2–3.

chapter six.   Positivists and the Manipulation of the Collective Imagination

1. The presence of mystic elements in Comte's work before he met Clotilde de Vaux is emphasized by Ernest Seillière, *Auguste Comte,* and Edward Caird, *The Social Philosophy and Religion of Comte.* The discontinuity between his earlier and later thought was in turn pointed out by Littré, one of his major followers, giving rise to the first great schism in positivism. John Stuart Mill, who sympathized with Comte's thought (to the point of organizing a fund in England to provide for his subsistence), also did not accept the philosopher's new phase. See John Stuart Mill, "Auguste Comte and Positivism," in *Collective Works of John Stuart Mill,* 10:261–368. On Comte in general, see Sybil de Acevedo et al., *Auguste Comte: Qui êtes-vous?*

2. Comte's positions after meeting Clotilde are expounded mainly in the *Catéchisme positiviste,* written in 1852, the most popular version dedicated especially to women, and in his *Système de politique positive, ou traité de sociologie instituant la religion de l'humanité,* written between 1851 and 1854.

3. Cited in R. Teixeira Mendes, *A mulher,* 32.

4. See Comte, *Système de politique positive,* 1:282.

5. Some of the ideas developed in this section were first expounded in my essay in *Revista do Brasil* 4, no. 8 (1989): 50–56, entitled "A ortodoxia positivista no Brasil: Um bolchevismo de classe média."

6. The accusation of sectarianism is found, for example, in Sílvio Romero, *Doutrina contra doutrina: O evolucionismo e o positivismo no Brasil.* The accusations by the orthodox positivists' most emotional enemies are exemplified by Antônio Torres in his work *Pasquinadas cariocas.* According to Torres, Teixeira Mendes "was truly a lunatic" (p. 140).

7. On positivism in Brazil generally, see Ivan Lins, *História do positivismo no Brasil;* Cruz Costa, *O positivismo na República: Notas sobre a história*

do positivismo no Brasil; and João Camilo de Oliveira Torres, *O positivismo no Brasil.*

8. A good part of the correspondence between Brazilian positivists and Pierre Laffitte has been published by Ivan Lins in *História do positivismo no Brasil.*

9. On this point, see Ernest Seillière, *Auguste Comte.*

10. Comte, *Appel aux conservateurs,* 109.

11. Letter of March 24, 1883, from Lemos to Laffitte. The list of duties of the members of the Positivist Society of Rio de Janeiro is found in Appendix E attached to the *Circulaire collective* of December 3, 1883. Besides forbidding the ownership of slaves and the acceptance of public office, it also included the duties of not exercising academic functions in institutions of higher learning, of not engaging in journalism for pay, and of signing one's name to all one's writings.

BIBLIOGRAPHY

Newspapers and Magazines

O Cruzeiro
O Diabo a Quatro
Diário de Notícias
Diário do Commercio
Diário Oficial
D. Quixote
O Filhote
Fon-Fon!
O Gato
Gazeta de Notícias
Jornal do Brasil
Jornal do Commercio
Kosmos
O Malho
O Mequetrefe
O Paiz
Revista do Arquivo Público Mineiro
Revista do Brasil
Revista do IHGB
Revista Illustrada
Semana Illustrada
O Tiradentes

Books

Acevedo, Sybil de, et al. *Auguste Comte: Qui êtes-vous?* [series]. Lyon: Manu-facture, 1988.

Agulhon, Maurice. *Marianne au combat: L'imagerie et la symbolique républi-caines de 1789 à 1880.* Paris: Flamarion, 1979.

Albuquerque, Medeiros e. *Quando eu era vivo.* Rio de Janeiro: Record, 1981.

Anais do Congresso Nacional de História da Propaganda, Proclamação e Consoli-dação da República no Brasil. 3 vols. Rio de Janeiro: IHGB, 1989.

Arendt, Hannah. *On Revolution.* New York: Viking Press, 1965.

Autos da devassa da Inconfidência Mineira. Rio de Janeiro: MEC–Biblioteca Nacional, 1936–48.

Baczko, Bronislaw. *Les imaginaires sociaux: Mémoires et espoirs collectifs.* Paris: Payot, 1984.

Banco do Brasil S.A. Museu e Arquivo Histórico. *Cédulas brasileiras da República: Emissões do Tesouro Nacional.* Rio de Janeiro, 1965.

Barbosa, Waldemar de Almeida. *A verdade sobre Tiradentes.* Belo Horizonte: Instituto de História, Letras e Arte, n.d.

Bernardes, Maria Thereza Caiuby Crescenti. *Mulheres de ontem? Rio de Janeiro—século XIX.* São Paulo: T. A. Queiroz, 1989.

Boal, Augusto, and Gianfrancesco Guarnieri. *Arena canta Tiradentes.* São Paulo: Sagarana, 1967.

Burton, Richard. *Viagem do Rio de Janeiro a Morro Velho.* Belo Horizonte: Itatiaia/Edusp, 1976.

Caird, Edward. *The Social Philosophy and Religion of Comte.* Glasgow: James Maclehore & Sons, 1885. New York: Kraus Reprint Co., 1969.

Campofiorito, Quirino. *História da pintura brasileira no século XIX.* Rio de Janeiro: Pinakotheke, 1983.

Cardoso, Vicente Licínio, ed. *À margem da história da República.* 2nd ed. Bra-sília: Câmara dos Deputados, 1981.

Carneiro, Paulo, ed. *Idéias políticas de Júlio de Castilhos.* Brasília: Senado Federal/FCRB, 1982.

Carvalho, José Murilo de. *Os bestializados: O Rio de Janeiro e a República que não foi.* São Paulo: Companhia das Letras, 1987.

Castro, A. R. Gomes de. *O monumento a Floriano por Eduardo de Sá.* Rio de Janeiro: Typographia Leuzinger, 1910.

Cavalcanti, Carlos. *Dicionário brasileiro de artistas plásticos.* 4 vols. Rio de Ja-neiro: INC, 1973–80.

Cintra, Francisco de Assis. *Tiradentes perante a história (revelações sobre a In-confidência Mineira).* São Paulo: Livraria do Globo, 1922.

Clark, T. J. *The Absolute Bourgeois: Artists and Politics in France, 1848–1851.* London: Thames and Hudson, 1982.

Coelho Netto. *Fogo fátuo.* Porto: Livraria Chardron de Lello e Irmão, 1929.

Comte, Auguste. *Appel aux conservateurs.* Paris: Chez l'Auteur et chez Victor Dalmont, 1855.

———. *Catéchisme positiviste.* Paris: Chez l'Auteur, 1852.

———. *Système de politique positive, ou traité de sociologie instituant la religion de l'humanité.* 4 vols. Osnabrück: Otto Zeller, 1967.

Constant, Benjamin. *De la liberté chez les modernes: Écrits politiques.* Textes présentés par M. Gauchet. Paris: Livre de Poche, 1980.

Correia, Leôncio. *A verdade histórica sabre o 15 de novembro.* Rio de Janeiro: Imprensa Nacional, 1939.

Correia, Serzedelo. *Páginas do passado.* Rio de Janeiro: Freitas Bastos, 1959.

Correia, Viriato. *Tiradentes: Comédia histórica em três atos e sete quadros.* Rio de Janeiro: Gráfica Guarany Ltda., 1941.

Costa, Cruz. *O positivismo na República: Notas sobre a história do positivismo no Brasil.* São Paulo: Cia. Editora Nacional, 1956.

Demolins, Edmond. *A quoi tient la supériorité des Anglo-Saxons.* Paris: Firmin-Didot et Cie, n.d.

Deodoro e a verdade histórica. Rio de Janeiro: Imprensa Nacional, 1937.

Duhet, Paule-Marie. *Les femmes et la Révolution, 1789–1794.* Paris: Gallimard, 1971.

Falcão, Aníbal. *Fórmula da civilização brasileira.* Rio de Janeiro: Ed. Guanabara, n.d.

Faraco, Sérgio. *Tiradentes: A alguma verdade (ainda que tardia).* Rio de Janeiro: Civilização Brasileira, 1980.

Freyre, Gilberto. *Ordem* e *progresso.* 3rd ed. 2 vols. Rio de Janeiro: José Olympio, 1974.

Girardet, Raoul. *Mitos e mitologias políticas.* São Paulo: Companhia das Letras, 1987.

Gottschalk, Louis Moreau. *Notes of a Pianist.* Edited by Jeanne Behrend. New York: Alfred A. Knopf, 1964.

Guimarães, Bernardo. *Histórias e tradições da província de Minas Gerais.* Rio de Janeiro: B. L. Garnier, 1872.

Hauser, Arnold. *The Social History of Art.* Vol. 3, *Rococo, Classicism, Romanticism.* New York: Vintage Books, 1985.

Hobsbawm, Eric J. *A invenção das tradições.* Rio de Janeiro: Paz e Terra, 1984.

Inconfidência Mineira, Revolução Francesa—200 Anos. Textos de Herculano Gomes Mathias e Maria do Carmo Dutra Lacombe. Rio de Janeiro: Caixa Econômica Federal/Spala Editora, 1989.

Jardim, Antônio da Silva. *Propaganda republicana (1888–1889).* Rio de Janeiro: MEC–Fundação Casa de Rui Barbosa, 1978.

Lange, Francisco Curt. *Vida y muerte de Louis Moreau Gottschalk en Río de Janeiro, 1869.* Mendoza: Universidad Nacional de Cuyo, 1951.

Leite, Miriam Lifchitz Moreira. *A mulher no Rio de Janeiro no século XIX*. São Paulo: Fundação Carlos Chagas, 1982.

Lima, Herman. *História da caricatura no Brasil*. 4 vols. Rio de Janeiro: Livraria José Olympio Editora, 1963.

Lima Júnior, Augusto de. *História da Inconfidência de Minas Gerais*. 3rd ed. Belo Horizonte: Itatiaia, 1968.

Lins, Ivan. *História do positivismo no Brasil*. 2nd ed. São Paulo: Cia. Editora Nacional, 1967.

Littré, Émile. *Auguste Comte et la philosophie positive*. Paris: Hachette, 1863.

Livro do centenário da Câmara dos Deputados (1826–1926). Rio de Janeiro: Assembléia Legislativa do Rio de Janeiro, 1986.

Magalhães Júnior, R. *Deodoro: A espada contra o Império*. 2 vols. São Paulo: Cia. Editora Nacional, 1957.

Marinho, José Antônio. *História da Revolução de 1842*. Brasília: Universidade de Brasília/Senado Federal, 1978.

Mathias, Herculano Gomes. *Tiradentes através da imagem*. Rio de Janeiro: Edições de Ouro, 1969.

Mendes, R. Teixeira [ed.]. *A bandeira nacional*. 3rd ed. Rio de Janeiro: Igreja Positivista do Brasil, 1958.

———. *Benjamin Constant: Esboço de uma apreciação sintética da vida e da obra do fundador da República brasileira*. 2nd ed. Rio de Janeiro: Apostolado Positivista do Brasil, 1913.

———. *A mulher: Sua preeminência social e moral segundo os ensinos da verdadeira ciência positiva*. Rio de Janeiro: Igreja e Apostolado Positivista do Brasil, 1958.

Mendes Fradique [pseud.]. *História do Brasil pelo método confuso*. Rio de Janeiro: Leite Ribeiro, 1922.

Miceli, Paulo. *O mito do herói nacional*. São Paulo: Contexto, 1988.

Monteiro, Tobias. *Pesquisas e depoimentos para a história*. Rio de Janeiro: Francisco Alves, 1913.

O monumento a Júlio de Castilhos. Governo do Estado do Rio Grande do Sul, 1922.

Moore, Barrington, Jr. *Social Origins of Dictatorship and Democracy: Lord and Peasant in the Making of the Modern World*. Boston: Beacon Press, 1967.

Moraes Filho, Mello. *Festas e tradições populares do Brasil*. Belo Horizonte: Edusp/Itatiaia, 1979.

Morse, Richard. *O espelho de Próspero: Cultura e idéias nas Américas*. São Paulo: Companhia das Letras, 1988.

Nettl, Paul. *National Anthems*. New York: Frederick Ungar Publishing Co., 1967.

Nicolet, Claude. *L'idée républicaine en France (1789–1924): Essai d'histoire critique*. Paris: Gallimard, 1982.

Pitkin, Hanna Fenichel. *The Concept of Representation.* Berkeley and Los Angeles: University of California Press, 1967.

Pompéia, Raul. *Obras.* Edited by Afrânio Coutinho. Vols. 7 and 8. Rio de Janeiro: Civilização Brasileira/Olac, 1983.

Porto, M. E. de Campos. *Apontamentos para a história da República dos Estados Unidos do Brasil.* Rio de Janeiro: Imprensa Nacional, 1890.

Prado, Eduardo. *A bandeira nacional.* São Paulo: Escola Typographica Salesiana, 1903.

———. *Fastos da ditadura militar no Brasil.* São Paulo: Escola Typographica Salesiana, 1902.

Priore, Mary del. *A mulher na história do Brasil.* São Paulo: Contexto, 1988.

Queiroz, Suely Robles Reis de. *Os radicais da República. Jacobinismo: Ideologia e ação, 1893–1897.* São Paulo: Brasiliense, 1986.

Ribeyrolles, Charles. *Brasil pitoresco.* Rio de Janeiro: Tipografia Nacional, 1859.

Romero, Silvio. *O Brasil social.* Rio de Janeiro: Typ. do Jornal do Commercio, 1907.

———. *Doutrina contra doutrina:* O *evolucionismo e o positivismo no Brasil.* Rio de Janeiro: Livraria Clássica de Alves e C., 1895.

Sahut, Marie-Catherine, and Michel Régis. *David: L'art et le politique.* Paris: Gallimard, 1988.

Santos, Lúcio José dos. *A Inconfidência Mineira.* 2nd ed. Belo Horizonte: Imprensa Oficial, 1972.

Seillière, Ernest. *Auguste Comte.* Paris: Félix Alcan, 1924.

Senna, Ernesto. *Deodoro: Subsídios para a história.* 2nd ed. Brasília: Universidade de Brasília, 1981.

Silva, Eduardo, ed. *Idéias políticas de Quintino Bocaiúva.* 2 vols. Senado Federal/Fundação Casa de Rui Barbosa, 1986.

———. *As queixas do povo.* Rio de Janeiro: Paz e Terra, 1988.

Silva, Hippolyto da. *Humorismos da propaganda republicana.* São Paulo: Duprat & Cia., 1904.

Silva, J. Norberto de Souza. *História da Conjuração Mineira.* Rio de Janeiro: B. L. Garnier, 1873.

Southey, Robert. *História do Brazil.* Translated by Luiz Joaquim de Oliveira Castro. 6 vols. Rio de Janeiro: Garnier, 1862.

Stourzh, Gerald. *Alexander Hamilton and the Idea of Republican Government.* Stanford: Stanford University Press, 1970.

Taunay, Visconde de. *Império e República.* São Paulo: Melhoramentos, n.d.

Taylor, Joshua C., ed. *Nineteenth-Century Theories of Art.* Berkeley, Los Angeles, and London: University of California Press, 1982.

Torres, Alberto. *A organização nacional.* 2nd ed. Rio de Janeiro: Cia. Editora Nacional, 1933.

Torres, Antônio. *Pasquinadas cariocas.* Rio de Janeiro: A. J. de Castilho Editor, 1921.

Torres, João Camilo de Oliveira. O *positivismo no Brasil.* Petrópolis: Vozes, 1943.

Uruguai, Visconde de. *Ensaio sabre o direito administrativo.* 2nd ed. Rio de Janeiro: Imprensa Nacional, 1960.

Viveiros, Esther de. *Rondon conta sua vida.* Rio de Janeiro: Livraria São José, 1958.

Whittlesey, E. S. *Symbols and Legends in Western Art: A Museum Guide.* New York: Scribner's Sons, 1972.

Articles, Chapters, Theses, Pamphlets

Agulhon, Maurice. "Esquisse pour une archéologie de la République: L'allégorie civique féminine." *Annales ESC* 28 (1973): 5–34.

Amaral, Ubaldino do. "Tiradentes." Address of April 21, 1894. Rio de Janeiro: n.p., 1906.

Araújo, José Pereira de. *Tiradentes.* Rio de Janeiro: Centro Positivista, 1884.

Barbosa, Francisco de Assis. "Para uma reavaliação de Floriano." In Sérgio Correa da Costa, *A diplomacia do marechal: Intervenção estrangeira na Revolta da Armada,* 2nd ed., xi–xxvi. Rio de Janeiro: Tempo Brasileiro/ Universidade de Brasília, 1979.

Barroso, Gustavo. "Os retratos de Tiradentes." *O Cruzeiro,* April 23, 1955.

Cardoso, Maria Helena Cabral de Almeida. "A herança arcaica do jacobinismo." Paper presented at the National Conference on the History of Propaganda, Proclamation and Consolidation of the Republic of Brazil. IHGB, November 1989.

Carelli, Mário. "Quelques réflexions autour de l'indéfinition de l'allégorie féminine du Brésil." *Cahiers du Brésil Contemporain,* Paris, Centre de Recherches sur le Brésil Contemporain, 12 (1990): 59–68.

Carvalho, José Murilo de. "Entre a liberdade dos antigos e a dos modernos: A República no Brasil." *Dados: Revista de Ciências Sociais* 32, no. 3 (1989): 265–80.

———. "Forças armadas e política, 1930–1945." In *A revolução de 30: Seminário internacional,* 109–50. Brasília: Universidade de Brasília/CPDOC, 1982.

———. "A ortodoxia positivista no Brasil: Um bolchevismo de classe média." *Revista do Brasil* 4, no. 8 (1989): 50–56.

Castro, Eduardo Machado de. "A Inconfidência Mineira: Narrativa popular." *Revista do Arquivo Publico Mineiro* 6, fasc. 1 (January–March, 1901): 1063–1151.

Castro Alves, Antônio Frederico de. "Gonzaga ou a revolução de Minas." In *Obras completas,* 579–661. Rio de Janeiro: Nova Aguilar, 1976.

Circulaire collective adressée à tous les vrais disciples d'Auguste Comte. Rio de Janeiro: Au Siège de la Société Positiviste, 1884.

"Conspiração em Minas Gerais no ano de 1789 para a Independência do Brasil." Article translated from Robert Southey, *História do Brasil,* by counselor José de Rezende Costa. *Revista do IHGB* 8 (1846): 297–310.

Costa, Maria Cristina Castilho. "O retrato feminino na pintura brasileira, 1800–1950." Master's thesis in anthropology, University of São Paulo, 1985.

Cotrim, Alvaro (Alvarus). "O 15 de novembro na imprensa ilustrada." *Jornal do Brasil,* November 15, 1973.

Donald, David. "The Folklore Lincoln." In Nicholas Cords and Patrick Forster, eds., *Myth and the American Experience,* 2:43–54. New York: Glencoe Press, 1973.

Fernandes, Rubem César. "Aparecida: nossa rainha, senhora e mãe, saravá!" In Viola Sachs et al., *Brasil & EUA: Religião e identidade nacional,* 85–111. Rio de Janeiro: Graal, 1988.

Fleiuss, Max. "Francisco Manuel da Silva e o hino nacional." Rio de Janeiro: Imprensa Nacional, 1917.

Girardet, Raoul. "Les trois couleurs, ni blanc, ni rouge." In Pierre Nora, ed., *Les lieux de mémoire,* vol. 1, *La République,* 7–35. Paris: Gallimard, 1984.

Guanabarino, Oscar. "O hino." O *Paiz,* January 21, 1890.

———. "O hino nacional." *O Paiz,* January 17, 1880.

Hobsbawm, Eric J. "Homem e mulher: imagens da esquerda." In *Mundos do Trabalho: Novos estudos sobre história operária,* 123–47. Rio de Janeiro: Paz e Terra, 1987. (Original English edition, Hobsbawm, *Worlds of Labour: Further Studies in the History of Labour.*)

Langlois, Claude. "Les dérives vendéennes et l'imaginaire révolutionaire." *Annales ESC* 3 (May–June 1988): 771–97.

Mariante, Helio Moro. "Revolução de 1893." Paper presented at the National Conference on the History of Propaganda, Proclamation and Consolidation of the Republic of Brazil. IHGB, November 1989.

Mello Júnior, Donato. "As primeiras exposições de belas artes na República." Paper presented at the National Conference on the History of Propaganda, Proclamation and Consolidation of the Republic of Brazil. IHGB, November 1989.

"Memória do êxito que teve a conjuração de Minas e dos factos relativos a ella acontecidos nesta cidade do Rio de Janeiro desde o dia 17 até 26 de abril de 1792." *Revista do IHGB* 62–63, t. 44 (1881): 140–60.

Mill, John Stuart. "Auguste Comte and Positivism." In *Collected Works of John Stuart Mill,* 10: 261–368. Toronto: University of Toronto Press, 1977.

Mourão, Ronaldo Rogério de Freitas. "A bandeira da República." *Revista do Brasil* 4, no. 8 (1989): 84–90.

Pinho, Wanderley. "A Questão Militar e a República." *Revista do Brasil* 2, no. 17 (November 1939): 23–30.

Pocock, J. G. A. "Civic Humanism and Its Role in Anglo-American Thought." In J. G. A. Pocock, *Politics, Language, and Time: Essays in Political Thought and History,* 80–103. New York: Atheneum, 1973.

Quinze de novembro: Contestação a Suetônio. Rio de Janeiro: n.p., 1898.

Roure, Agenor de. "A bandeira nacional." *Kosmos* 4, no. 3 (March 1907).

Sales, Alberto. "Balanço político: Necessidade de uma reforma constitucional." *Estado de São Paulo,* July 18 and 25, 1901.

Silva, J. Norberto de Souza. "O Tiradentes perante os historiadores oculares de seu tempo." *Revista do IHGB* 62–63, t. 44 (1881): 131–39.

Thomé Júnior. "Já é tempo!" *Revista Ilustrada,* no. 590 (May 1890): 2–3.

Tiradentes: Homenagem ao primeiro mártir da liberdade. Ouro Preto, Tip. do Liberal Mineira, 1888.

"Últimos momentos dos inconfidentes de 1789 pelo frade que os assistiu de confissão." *Revista do IHGB* 62–63, t. 44 (1881): 161–86.

Vovelle, Michel. "La marseillaise: La guerre ou la paix." In Pierre Nora, ed., *Les lieux de mémoire,* vol. 1, *La République,* 85–136. Paris: Gallimard, 1984.

INDEX

ABOUT THE AUTHOR

José Murilo de Carvalho, born in 1939, holds a Ph.D. in political science from Stanford University (1975). He was appointed a professor at the Federal University of Minas Gerais and later professor at the Federal University of Rio de Janeiro. He has been a visiting professor at Stanford University; the University of California, Irvine; the University of Notre Dame; Oxford University; the University of London; the University of Leiden; and the School for Advanced Studies in the Social Sciences in Paris (EHESS). He was a visiting fellow at the Institute for Advanced Study at Princeton University. He is a member of the Brazilian Academy of Letters, the Brazilian Academy of Sciences, and the Brazilian Historical and Geographical Institute. He has published 12 books and nearly 120 articles in academic journals in Brazil and around the world. Among his most prominent books are *A construção da ordem* (1980), *Teatro de sombras* (1988), *Os bestializados: O Rio de Janeiro e a República que não foi* (1987), and *Cidadania ano Brasil: O longo caminho* (2001). His most recent book is the biography *D. Pedro II: Ser ou não ser* (2007).